Sassy,
SINGLE,
& SATISFIED

Michelle McKinney Hammond

HARVEST HOUSE™ PUBLISHERS

EUGENE, OREGON

Cover by Koechel Peterson & Associates, Inc., Minneapolis, Minnesota

Cover photo by Ernest Collins

Published in association with the literary agency of Alive Communications, Inc., 7680 Goddard Street, Suite 200, Colorado Springs, CO 80920

SASSY, SINGLE, AND SATISFIED
Copyright © 2003 by Michelle McKinney Hammond
Published by Harvest House Publishers
Eugene, Oregon 97402

Library of Congress Cataloging-in-Publication Data

McKinney Hammond, Michelle, 1957-
  Sassy, single, and satisfied / Michelle McKinney Hammond.
     p. cm.
  ISBN 0-7369-0487-5 (pbk.)
     1. Single women—Religious life. 2. Christian women—Religious life. I. Title.
BV4596.S5 .S347 2003
248.8'432—dc21   2002014462

Printed in the United States of America.

03 04 05 06 07 08 09 10 11 / VP-KB / 10 9 8 7 6 5 4

Lady, this is for you. For all the sisters who have questioned, prayed, cried in the middle of the night, and discussed for endless hours with their closest inner circle how to endure this thing called being alone. I feel for you, I've walked in your shoes, and I'm here to tell you there is a dance you can do to the beat of one. Take heart and be encouraged.

Thank You, Lord. You have been a faithful Lover like no other because You are the Lover of my Soul. There is no one like You. There are no words to express the love and joy I feel inside at the mere thought of You.

ACKNOWLEDGMENTS

To all of those who have been faithful encouragers through my own struggles with singleness: Bunny, Terri, Denise, my faithful twelve. There's no way to leave anyone out because you all know who you are. I've told you a thousand times! (smile)

Harvest House: Bob, Carolyn, LaRae, Julie, Betty, Barb, Shana, Teresa, Brynn, and all who so diligently work with me. Because you are, I am. I never take that for granted. I love and appreciate you beyond expression. I am so glad that we are family and I get to live and work at your house!

CONTENTS

Introduction

God has a sense of humor. The day I picked up a copy of *Today's Christian Woman* magazine and read the front page with my picture blown up on it, larger than life, reading "Michelle McKinney Hammond: Why She's Sassy, Single, and Satisfied," well, I just hollered. I mean laughter rolled from the deepest part of my belly, and I said, "God, You are so funny!" This was our private joke. We both knew there was a day, there was a time when I was sassy. Oh yes! Single? Most definitely. But satisfied? Absolutely not!

I lived in a place called Overwhelming Misery. Finally, one day as I sat in my room, mulling over my misfortune at being single, I became so exasperated I shook my puny fist at God and loudly declared, "Lord, I am so sick and tired of being sick and tired that I'm issuing You a challenge. I don't want You to give me a mate until You can prove to me that I can be happy with just You! Right now I don't believe it, and I want You to prove it to me. I'm not feeling the love, Jesus. I need You to show me something or I'm just going to have to chuck this whole being saved bit and go back to life as it was before I met You, because frankly I'm not feeling any different. The only difference between then and now is that I am living holy and alone. At least I had a man before, whether his intentions toward me were good or not!"

Well, what did I say that for?

God quietly said, "Okay," and proceeded to take me on the journey of a lifetime. A tour through His heart...and wow, I came out on the other side completely elated…downright sassy, single, and satisfied.

So many have asked me, *"Michelle, how did you get to be so happy? I mean, don't you want to get married?"* Of course I do! *"Don't you want to be loved and touched and held and, well…you know?"* Ooh, don't get me started! All of that and more! But since that is not where I presently live, I can't wait until then to live life to the fullest. That would be like saying I have to wait until I have a man to eat, dress, or live a comfortable life. And that most *definitely* is not going on. If that was the case I would be emaciated or dead by now! No, ladies, we've all decided to take care of ourselves the best way we can. The difference between us is that some are actually *enjoying* themselves while others are merely existing. Waiting to exhale. How can you hold your breath that long? Go ahead, let it out. Waiting for what you term your "other half" or "better half" to show up, complete your life, and crown you with joy is not the answer to abundant living.

If a man is what you are waiting for to rock your world and make you dance to a joyful rhythm, it will never happen. Even if that man shows up. Why? Because all you will learn by what you acquire is that none of the things you were waiting for is able to give you the joy you've been looking for.

What is the secret for getting to a place called happy, content, fulfilled, and downright joyful? How do you qualify for loving the life you're living? Hang with me for a time and I'll share the meditations and discoveries that got me there. Take my word for it 'cause I've been there, done that "when will I ever be truly happy" thing, and come out the better for it. Hopefully what I have to share will get you on the right road. So buckle up and get ready for the trip. We're getting ready to go some places. You won't like all the scenery you see, but that's all right. It's called going through to get where you really want to be. You can make it. I know, 'cause I've already visited those same stops, took pictures for the sake of understanding a thing or two, and made it to the other side. I suggest you do likewise…well, what are you waiting for? Hurry up, girl, 'cause I'm waiting for you!

Once Upon a Time

Once upon a time there was a woman called Lonely. Her desperate search for love led her to places that were not her intention. Down the River of Tears to the Valley of Humiliation. Through the endless Plains of Depression to the Field of Shame. Deeper and deeper inside of herself she went until she could no longer see the Forest of Joy that was set before her, so distracted was she by the trees of her own desires. At times, she would come to a place called Blame where she struggled to find the source of her senseless mistakes. At times, she felt like she had been walking in circles, as she had visited this place often. Then a gentle voice would call to her, "Continue to travel until you find the answer to your dreams. It is close at hand."

Onward she traveled, sometimes believing she had reached an oasis only to discover that it was a mirage. But lost in the desert of her passions, she had no choice but to move on until she found refreshment for her parched soul. On and on she went. Sometimes running, sometimes walking, sometimes struggling to put one foot in front of the other—until she faced a dead end. Realizing that she had come to the end of herself, she finally looked up and from the hills, her help came. Strong and gentle, lifting her out of the abyss of her own loneliness. Surrounding her with a comfort she'd never known. She finally realized she was right back where she had started looking...into the eyes of the One who had always loved her.

"Where have you been?" He said, already knowing the answer.

"Looking for love," she replied.

"I am He," the stranger answered.

"You look so familiar," she said, searching the recesses of her heart for a remembrance of the day and the time when they first met.

"I have always known you and loved you." His smile haunted her and stirred sweet feelings within. "What is your name?" He softly whispered.

"My name is… my name is…," her voice trailed off as she forgot herself, so caught up in Him was she. The longing was gone, replaced by His all-consuming love. The memory of who she had been in Him, long before she became distracted by other lovers and empty promises, returned. Catching her reflection in His eyes, her answer was music to her own ears. "My name is Beloved," she said.

With all your getting,

       get an understanding

For understanding releases you

       to embrace the truth

And that truth

       will equip you

          to be released

             into the arms

                of joyful,

                   victorious living….

Meditations on Life...

sas·sa·fras \'sas-(ə-),fras\ *n* [Sp *sasafrás*] (1577)   **1** : a tall eastern No. American tree (*Sassafras albidum*) of the laurel family with mucilaginous twigs and leaves   **2** : the dried root bark of the sassafras used esp. as a diaphoretic or flavoring agent

¹Sas·sa·ni·an *or* **Sa·sa·ni·an** \sə-'sä-nē-ən, sa-'sä-\ *adj* (1788) : of, relating to, or having the characteristics of the Sassanid dynasty of ancient Persia or its art or architecture

²Sassanian *or* **Sasanian** *n* (1855) : SASSANID

Sas·sa·nid \sə-'sän-əd, -'san-; 'sas-ⁿn-\ *n* [NL *Sassanidae* Sassanids, fr. *Sassan*, founder of the dynasty] (1776) : a member of a dynasty of Persian kings of the 3d to 7th centuries — **Sassanid** *adj*

sass·wood \'sas-,wùd\ *n* [earlier *sassywood*, fr. *sassy* sasswood + *wood*] (1897) : a western African leguminous tree (*Erythrophloeum guineënse*) with a poisonous bark and a hard strong insect-resistant wood

Sassy /'sas-ē/ adj. 1: SAUCY 2: VIGOROUS, LIVELY 3: distinctively smart and stylish.

satch·el \'sach-əl\ *n* [ME *sachel*, fr. MF, fr. L *saccellus*, dim. of *saccus* bag — more at SACK] (14c) : a small bag often with a shoulder strap ⟨schoolboys with their ∼*s*⟩ — **satch·el·ful** \-,fùl\ *n*

¹sate \'sät, 'sat\ *archaic past of* SIT

²sate \'sät\ *vt* **sat·ed; sat·ing** [prob. by shortening & alter. fr. *satiate*] (1602)   **1** : to cloy with overabundance : GLUT   **2** : to appease (as a thirst) by indulging to the full   **syn** see SATIATE

sa·teen \sa-'tēn, sə-\ *n* [alter. of *satin*] (1878) : a smooth durable lustrous fabric usu. made of cotton in satin weave

sat·el·lite \'sat-ᵊl-,īt\ *n* [MF, fr. L *satellit-, satelles* attendant] (1548)   **1** : a hired agent or obsequious follower : MINION, SYCOPHANT   **2 a** : a celestial body orbiting another of larger size   **b** : a man-made object or vehicle intended to orbit the earth, the moon, or another celestial body   **3** : someone or something attendant, subordinate, or dependent; *esp* : a country politically and economically dominated or controlled by another more powerful country   **4** : a usu. independent urban community situated near but not immediately adjacent to a large city — **satellite** *adj*

Start with Surrender

*Getting wisdom is the most important thing you can do!
And whatever else you do, get good judgment.*

PROVERBS 4:7 NLT

Exactly what have you got? And what do you understand so far about life, love, and men? And especially about yourself? Let's look at your collection. Hmmm, sad love stories of the one who got away. Romances that almost were, or endless days spent alone wondering why? Experiences that made you wiser, if not older. A laundry list of questions for when you finally have a throne-room, face-to-face conversation with God. Oh, but what have we here? A gem tucked away in the corner of your treasure chest. Surrender.

That's it. Surrender to the sovereignty of God. Whether you believe it or not, God is still in control. He has every single one of your days written in His book, and according to His calculations, you won't arrive a day later or earlier than what has been scheduled. Try to scoot ahead of the program, and you will experience a setback—a nudge back to where you should be. Try to lag behind, and you will find yourself learning things in a course you didn't know you signed up for. Take it from me. In the end God always has His way. Surrender to His ways and learn your lessons the easy way.

Understanding His heart toward you and His will for your life is critical to your heart condition. What you believe will color all your decisions. You will either rest in His plan or make

painful choices because you feel you have no other options—
anything goes. In this instance, *something* becomes better than
nothing. There couldn't possibly be a bigger lie than that rationale for settling beneath your calling. Understand that, in God's
economy, you will always have choices. His desire is for you to
be in the position to make the best ones.

What else should you understand? Understand that He
loves you. He wants the best for you. He hears you. He wants
you to be happy and complete. He has a plan. He's working it
out for you. So wait on the Lord and be of good courage. He
will strengthen your heart for the duration until He delivers
your deepest desires. In the meantime, understand that no matter how you feel, this isn't about your feelings. It is bigger than
that. It is about His divine plan for your life. And *dahling*, it is
simply fabulous! Just wait, you'll see.

Daily Bread

Man does not live by bread alone, but by every word that proceeds from the mouth of God...

MATTHEW 4:4 RSV

*W*hat exactly does this have to do with me being happy? you might be thinking. This is where we must start. What is bread? Here, Jesus is talking about physical bread, which sustains us. We can take this one step further. Bread is whatever we *think* sustains us. Food, love, achievements, money, material things that make us feel better about ourselves...you name it. You fill in the blanks. What does it take to bring you satisfaction? To put a smile on your face? To make you say, "Hey, I'm feeling pretty good about myself?"

Now trash that list. It will never be enough. We've seen them. People who have everything and yet they are still miserable. They still have days when they scratch their heads and wonder, *Is this all there is to life?* Now, mind you, that might be hard for us to imagine, but catch any of them on the right day and you will see the hint of secret longings and unfulfilled desires lurking in the shadows of their eyes. Why? Because after all is said and done, our relationship with God and the trust we have in His promises are what truly sustains us. Through the good, the bad, and the ugly, His Word is the foundation of our peace and fulfillment.

I had to learn how to personalize the Word of God for myself in order to draw comfort and instruction from it. So for the sake of where I want to take you, I will be sharing the things He has taught me. Now for those of you who are religious, I'm not adding a jot or a tittle to the Word; I'm simply making it plain for where you really live. God never designed His Word to be so spiritual that it would be of no earthly good. After all, He knows that we are "mere dust" and knows the way we work. He wants to get real with us, if you know what I mean. So let's get down to the nitty-gritty on what we need to know to get happy, okay?

Buried Treasures

*Those who cling to worthless idols forfeit the grace
that could be theirs…*

JONAH 2:8

*A*s Jonah sat in the belly of the great fish, he had a lot of time to collect his thoughts. I, too, have been consumed by my desires and found them overwhelming to the point that I forgot how blessed I presently was. Things that should have brought me joy were ignored as I considered all that I wanted and still didn't have. They were worthless idols, only promising joy but not delivering. Can you relate?

Hmmm…What are worthless idols? All of the things that we think will make us happy. All the things that we believe are the answer to a contented life. Have you ever seen an outfit or a piece of jewelry that you just *had* to have? You saved your shekels religiously for it, and finally the day came when the thrill of making that item yours became a reality. You enjoyed it. Showed it off to your friends. Wore it proudly. Then one day you saw something else, and you put your treasure in the closet or your jewelry box and became caught up in the pursuit of the new acquisition. Perhaps you even forgot you had the original thing until you decided to spring clean and rediscovered it. I'm guilty, too. Ah, how quickly the romance dies…why? Why can't we ever be satisfied? Because most of the things we long after are temporal…in the end, pretty worthless. I believe God wants us to learn that everything in life is temporary except His awesome love for us. It is the one thing that will never lose its luster.

What is the grace that slips through our fingers as we pursue what we think we want? Present joy. Present fulfillment. Blessings overlooked because we are too focused on the one thing we can't have. We walk right past friendships rich with promise, career opportunities, places not traveled to, new experiences never tried, little loving arms that long to be held just as much as we do…are you getting the picture?

So many times we put off for tomorrow what should be done today. Today's treasures are buried under our longing for what we think tomorrow will bring. How typical of the enemy of our souls to keep us distracted from the present by binding us to worrying about our future! Here is the bottom line: Today is today. It comes complete with its own set of joys and mini-dramas. Leave tomorrow alone; it will come soon enough. For now, choose to embrace what is available and possible and enjoy it. Choose to live in the moment and collect wonderful memories. After all, in the end all you will have is your remembrance of yesterday once the next day dawns. You will either live to regret it or celebrate it. The choice is yours.

Forbidden Fruit

Now the serpent was more crafty than any of the wild animals the LORD God had made. He said to the woman, "Did God really say, `You must not eat from any tree in the garden'?"

GENESIS 3:1

*W*hy do we feel that if we are not married we are not free to enjoy life to the fullest? There is a rampant disease in Christendom called, "One-Tree-I-Tis." It is when we focus on the one tree that we can't have at the moment to the point we fail to see all the trees we can enjoy. So we put every area of our life on hold as we gaze at that one tree that seems out of reach. The serpent slithers up to us and asks a misleading question. "You mean to tell me that God is going to rob you of enjoying your life? How cruel is that?" Don't fall for it! God wants you to enjoy life. But you won't if you keep staring at that one tree.

Take a look around you. At all that you have access to. Touch, taste, enjoy, savor. The flavor might change tomorrow. Don't get caught up in what you don't have and superimpose your sense of lack over all that is readily available to you. Get the right perspective. Take another look. What do you see? Loving friends, interesting activities, new things to learn and experience…the list of trees that you can select fruit from grows ever longer once you get over yourself and look beyond where you presently stand. Be adventurous. Dare to enjoy what is available. Throw your longings to the wind and allow them to settle on God's altar. Perhaps He wants you to sample the other flavors of life before serving you a more predictable diet.

Is God really telling you not to enjoy your life to the fullest? I think not!

Mind Games

He [Jesus] ate nothing during those days, and at the end of them he was hungry. The devil said to him, "If you are the Son of God, tell this stone to become bread."

LUKE 4:2-3

Truly, when we are hungry, we are easy prey for the devil. When we are starving for love, he comes to question our identity and challenge us to provide for ourselves. Thoughts assault our minds...*If God really loved you, wouldn't He give you what you desire so deeply? Perhaps you've waited long enough; why don't you just get it for yourself? Get off the goody-two-shoes act. Nice girls finish last. You've got to make things happen for yourself. Faith without works is dead. What are you waiting for?* Blah, blah, blah...we've all been there and know the lines by heart.

Dangerous dialogue can invite more heartache if we don't stay centered. Don't let your hunger distract you and start playing mind games with your spirit. Know, just as Jesus knew, that you are a child of God and have a loving Father who only has your best in mind. All blessings come from His hand. You never know what you are getting if you conjure something up on your own. When we move out of time or out of season, we forfeit the protection of God over our lives as well as our hearts. Therefore, be still and know that He is God. Perhaps we don't understand why He does what He does or why He takes so long, but still He knows best and He is sovereign. Stand fast in your faith, and don't give in to the fear that your hunger will never be satisfied. Lack is for a season and then comes lasting fulfillment, but only in God's perfect time after you have endured the tests and preparation. Just as Jesus was being prepared for a work in the wilderness, you are being prepared to receive your blessings. The time of patient endurance is what will qualify you to not only recognize but receive your blessing. Hold fast my sister, for after you have done the will of the Father, He that will come, will come and not tarry.

Perfect Timing

When Rachel saw that she was not bearing Jacob any children, she became jealous of her sister. So she said to Jacob, "Give me children, or I'll die!" Jacob became angry with her and said, "Am I in the place of God, who has kept you from having children?"

GENESIS 30:1-2 NLT

While they were still some distance from Ephrath, Rachel began to give birth and had great difficulty. And as she was having great difficulty in childbirth, the midwife said to her, 'Don't be afraid, for you have another son.' As she breathed her last—for she was dying—she named her son Ben-Oni. But his father named him Benjamin. So Rachel died and was buried on the way to Ephrath (that is, Bethlehem)" (Genesis 35:16-19).

Hmmm, this causes pause for thought. Jacob asks a good question. Is a mate or a child in the place of God in your heart? Perhaps this is the cause of delay. God is a jealous lover who will not share His place as your first love with anyone or anything else. Perhaps it's time to place things in the right order in your heart.

The second thought that must be considered as we consider the outcome of when Rachel finally receives her request is this: Perhaps God knows that the thing you think you can't live without is the very thing that will kill you. Kill your joy.

Kill the possibilities for an incredible life. Again, trust Him with
the seasons of your life. Embrace each season with joy, in the
full confidence that God knows what's best for your life today,
tomorrow, and forever...

Just Your Size

But seek first the kingdom of God and His righteousness,
and all these things shall be added to you.

MATTHEW 6:33 NKJV

How many times have we all heard that scripture and gotten upset? "Seek first the kingdom of God..." We've heard it enough to find it trite, but it is still true. Our focus is all wrong. Our priorities are a bit askew. It's like buying the accessories before you get the basic outfit. How will you know if they go together or complement one another? If you don't know God's will for your life, how will you know who fits into His plan?

Perhaps we force the issue because we don't want to deal with the real issue. It's like trying to put on a dress that is too small. We try to squeeze into it instead of doing the work it would take to make it fit comfortably on its own. How about changing our diet? Losing a little weight? Working out so we're the right size for that gorgeous little number? The truth of the matter is when we are ready, and if it's in accord with God's will, the things we long for will come. They fall into place and fit into our lives just right. A woman at peace with her God, content with her life, full of love, and free of desperation attracts a good man. It starts and ends with us. It's time to take stock of our priorities. What is truly important in this thing we call the single life?

Is it really about a man? Or is it about being a whole person? Which brings us to another thought. Why are we really here? Is it just to get married and become the extension of someone else or is it for something greater? Just asking!

First things first, ladies. Your God-given purpose will not be reliant on another person. You are called to build a good life complete in Christ. Then you will know God's rich blessings in your life—whatever they may be.

Live a little,

Laugh even more,

Embrace the wind,

Kiss the sky,

Dare to dream,

Smell a flower,

And remind yourself

Life is bigger than what you can hold.

Pure Pleasure

And for thy [God's] pleasure they are and were created.
REVELATION 4:11 KJV

I hear you, I hear you. *But what do I get out of the deal? He gets all the pleasure, what do I get?* Any smart woman knows that if you treat a good man, not just any man, but a good man like a king, he is sure to treat you like a queen. It is the law of reciprocity. Truly God is no different. We've got to get past the vending machine mentality that if we stick in a good prayer or a religious duty, God will shoot down the prize of our choice. Uh-uh, it ain't happenin'. Yes, I said *ain't* for added emphasis. Back to basics, ladies. God created man and woman because *He* wanted company. *He* wanted someone to fellowship with. He wanted someone to worship Him and give Him admiration for His creation. In exchange, Adam and Eve got all the perks of a fabulous life. An incredible place to live, free food, and each other. No bills, no drama, not even bad weather! All they had to do was love God and enjoy His visits while keeping an eye on everything in the Garden. Sounds simple enough to me.

But could Adam and Eve appreciate a good thing? Noooo! They had to blow it by taking their focus off of God in pursuit of something they didn't need. I often wonder, what exactly did Eve want to know? Anyway, it couldn't possibly have been greater than what God was already telling them, but that sly snake convinced them that God was holding out on them.

Can you relate? Do you feel as though God is holding out on you by not giving you your mate? Don't go for the okey-doke. It's a smoke screen for absolutely nothing. You know even the right mate at the wrong time can turn into a nightmare. Remember: God is in the habit of handing out good and perfect gifts, not half-baked cookies that will make you sick.

A la *Young's Literal Translation of the Bible.* Eve even confessed, after being confronted by God, that the serpent had deceived her and caused her to forget! Forget what?! Forget that she was sublimely happy until the serpent showed up to convince her otherwise? Forget that God had already given her everything her heart desired? Forget that God was good, and whatever she didn't have perhaps He already knew she didn't need it? Or could it be that she forgot who she was and why she was created in the first place? Ouch! I think I heard some toes being stepped on.

Contrary to what the serpent suggests, God is not selfish. He is completely justified in wanting what He wants after all that He has done for us. Plus it behooves you to keep your heart in the right place for your own protection. Still wondering what we get out of the deal when we seek to please God first? We get pleased in return. When we seek to please ourselves, all we get is frustrated. The more we gain, the more joy we lose as we find all that we acquire leads to greater emptiness. We were made to worship Him not just in a song on Sunday mornings, but 24/7 in all that we say and do. When God knows He finally has all of you—heart, soul, mind, and strength—He can give you the desires of your heart and trust you not to idolize them. True worshipers are able to keep their blessings in perspective. Giver first, gift second.

Are you there yet? Or are you still acting like an opera singer who cries, "me, me, me!" Hurry up and destroy that soundtrack so you can get to the good part of the movie. The first secret to being a good lover and getting the love you want is not to be selfish. A good lover makes sure the beloved is pleased first because he or she understands that giving pleasure begets pleasure. For now, remember it's not about you, girlfriend, it's all about Him. When you get your heart priorities in order, the pleasure will be all His to please you back. Can you say "pretty please"?

Celebrate Your Gifts

And God blessed them, and God said to them,
"Be fruitful and multiply, and fill the earth and subdue it;
and have dominion over…every living thing
that moves upon the earth."

GENESIS 1:28 RSV

You've heard me say it before, and I'll say it again. Contrary to popular belief, the hole in our hearts is not a person-sized whole. This can be confirmed by many a married person who wakes up on any given morning and gazes at their mate while thinking, *You are not making me happy.* Certainly this can be a disappointing revelation if the perception was that marriage was the answer to the joy factor. But deep in their hearts, after they've said "I do," an inner voice urges them not to put all their eggs in one basket because there is more to life than marriage. The "more" keeps calling them to come and discover it. They struggle to shake off the haunting voice that whispers, "There must be more to life than this," feeling guilty even at the thought. "After all, I should be happy with this person." But the truth of the matter is, having a partner without purpose is an empty life.

The void that nags us most is the vast chasm that waits to be filled with our purpose, our calling, the reason we were created. Before Adam received a mate, God gave him his purpose. He said, "Go forth and conquer, take dominion over your world. Don't let life give you the run around, I am giving you the authority to reel it in and run it." After Adam set about fulfilling his assignment, God decided he needed help. So you think God is not aware of your needs? Perhaps He has a better handle on them than you do. If you are not busy fulfilling the purpose you were created for, why do you need a partner? You don't need help feeling sorry for yourself; you can do that on your own time.

So how do we get God to decide it's time to add the dimension of partnership to our lives? By fulfilling the first requirement—our purpose, to worship Him first, then be fruitful in every area of our lives. Using our gifts to bless others, being excellent at work, touching the lives of people around us. Multiplying good works so that others around us see them and glorify our Father in heaven.

But Michelle, I don't know what my purpose is. Your purpose is to exploit your gifts to bless others. *But I don't know what my gift is!* Let me help you. Your gift is the thing that everyone celebrates about you, though you may take it for granted. The reason it's no big deal to you is because it's your natural gift. It is inherent to your nature to be creative, detail-oriented, good with children, sharp with numbers, given to hospitality, an effective counselor …whatever it is, God wants you to use your God-given abilities to bless others around you. In the process, you will prosper. Not just materially, but emotionally and spiritually. You will be filled with the satisfaction of knowing that you live a life that matters to God, others, and even yourself. There is no greater sense of joy and peace than to lay your head down at the end of the day knowing that you were used to help someone, to add something to someone else's life. And if you're getting paid for it, well, that's even better!

I believe that some people are unhappy at their jobs because they are not doing what they were created to do. Somewhere along the line, they didn't figure out how to make their natural gift marketable and settled for a job where they learned what was termed a "practical skill." Well, it may be practical, but is it natural to you? It's like asking a fish to breathe out of water. In its natural environment, it flourishes and moves freely, but on land it merely gasps for life.

Many of us are gasping for life and thinking that life is found in another. Not true. True life begins with you living your life with purpose.

I drink from life

and find its flavor sweet and mysterious

Sometimes burning my tongue

filling me with shivers of delight

restlessly bubbling inside of me

It is a myriad of tastes

No one standing out alone

Hints of happiness, sadness

Peace, turmoil

Doubt, faith

Resignation and hope

Feed me, refresh me

Revive me

And urge me to try again

to take another sip

tomorrow…

Life in the Garden

The Lord God planted all sorts of beautiful trees there in the garden, trees producing the choicest of fruit. At the center of the garden he placed the Tree of Life, and also the Tree of Conscience, giving knowledge of Good and Bad.

GENESIS 2:9 TLB

When we come to know the Lord, we enter His Garden. The Garden implies our exit from the world and our entrance into kingdom living. The word Eden means "pleasure" or "delight." Kingdom living is supposed to give us pleasure. When we enter into this dimension of life, we have a lot at our disposal. Trees producing the choicest of fruit, the best of everything within your reach and yours for the picking. What will you choose? Will you waste time trying to gain knowledge that will only lead to your dissatisfaction or will you eat of life to the fullest?

What is the life that we should be eating? All the rich experiences that life has to offer. Don't put life on hold while you wait for a mate. Now is the time to experiment. Take that class. Go on that trip. Make that investment. Try something new. Laugh loudly. Paint a wall red. Go for it! No one will make your life happen but you. Make it interesting. Break your everyday routine. Mix it up. Go to an art exhibit after work. Check out a play. Take a cooking class. (Oops! I'm not trying to hurt anybody's feelings; however, you fill in the blank.) What I'm saying is that most of the time we are bored with life because *we* are boring. Most of us just go to work, go to church, and go home. That is not living life. That is going through the motions of an empty existence. There is nothing intriguing or exciting about predictability—it's time to break your present mold.

Use your imagination and do something you've never done before. God wants you to taste life, to sample all the goodies He has made available. Venture out. See His creation. Notice something you've never noticed before. It's amazing how alive you will feel as you abandon your comfort zone for a new adventure. Remember, for everything you've never done before it is because *you've* chosen not to do it before, not because you couldn't. Make different choices. Break your normal routine. Don't wait for anyone else. Get a life. Be a pioneer. Get out there and live it up!

Time Out

Let me ask you a question...

What is something that you've always wanted to do, yet never have?

What is stopping you from doing it?

What would it take to get you going?

Is there something that you can do right now to begin doing what you want to do?

Do you have someone to keep you accountable?

Make a date with yourself to begin.

And what about those gifts, girlfriend?

What would you gladly do if you could get paid for it?

What would you do if you could do it for free and still survive?

What steps can you take to begin to do what makes you happy?

What type of plan would you need to position yourself to make a career change to use your gifts?

Is there something you can do part-time until you've built up enough funds to make a change?

Make a plan and work it. Give yourself a date to begin.

Double Delight

But he (Elkanah) gave Hannah a special portion because he loved her very much, even though the Lord had given her no children.

1 SAMUEL 1:5 NLT

The story goes that Hannah was married to a man named Elkanah who also had another wife, Peninah. Peninah had children, Hannah had none. Peninah lorded this fact over Hannah, especially when they went to worship. She would provoke poor Hannah to irritate her. It bothered poor Hannah so that she became depressed and stopped eating. Sound familiar? Yet her husband still loved her greatly, and gave her a double portion. Let's personalize the scripture. "But to you the Lord has given a special portion because He loves you even though you may wonder why you don't have what you want yet." Another translation says a double portion, perhaps it was even more, all I know is that we, like Hannah, can either consider what we don't have or look at what we have been given.

Satan wants to destroy your countenance so that you cannot worship God. He wants you to focus on what you *don't* have so that you can't enjoy what you *do* have. Don't miss this major truth that should make you dance, shout, and praise your Savior. God has also given you a double portion of blessing! You have double the time because it's all yours to do with as you please, without having to check with anyone else. You have double the money to spend because it's all yours; you don't have to split it with anyone! Double the space to stretch out and fill your world with all that you want in it. Double the resources to explore purposeful living. Enjoy it while you can.

And by all means don't sit around looking all down in the mouth. Eat something! Sample all the goodies life offers. Don't put life on hold waiting for someone else to complete it. Savor every day as if it is your last and squeeze every single drop out of it. Remember, tomorrow is not promised. What can you do to enjoy yourself today? Do it! Do it with gusto. When Hannah got refocused on God and His priorities, she offered the desire of her heart back to God. She sacrificed her longings and received a precious promise from the Lord through the priest Eli. On that note, she changed her countenance. She ate, she worshipped, and she became fruitful. However, when she received what she desired, she was quick to give it back to God and remain focused on the Giver above the gift. God honored her for this in a marvelous way. The desires of her heart were fulfilled beyond measure with not just one child, but five more!

What are you eating? Are you digesting the promises of God? Are you consuming all that life has to offer? If not, check your diet, girl! Start a new regime and then get your praise on!

Designer Original

Who told you that you were naked? Did you eat from the tree I commanded you not to eat?

GENESIS 3:11 NLT

You know, if you're not careful, you'll eat all the wrong things. Little lies about every thing that you are not. You are too fat, too skinny, too short, too tall, too quiet, too loud. Not gifted. Unlovable, undesirable. Not worthy of anything good and lasting. Destined to be unhappy for the rest of your life. On and on…you fill in the blanks.

Yes, you will be strolling through life minding your own business and the devil will sidle up to you and point out all the things you don't have. He will taunt you and tell you that God has been holding out on you and get you to digest his prefabricated lies. Once you've partaken of one lie, all the rest of them begin to sound good and reasonable. Before you know it, you've moved ahead of God, grabbed at life and all you want for yourself, only to find you made a big mistake. By the time God finds you hiding behind the bush of your own shame, all you will be able to reply is, "I heard You coming and I hid myself so that You wouldn't see my nakedness. My undone state. I'm so embarrassed, God." Then will come the question: "But who told you that you were naked? Who told you that you were undesirable? Destined to a life of unfulfillment? Incomplete? Not whole? I never told you that. Why would you believe such a lie?"

Why would you? God calls you "Beloved," "Married," "Set apart for His divine purpose." Whether you believe that or not, it's a settled issue in His mind. Settle it in your mind, too. The reality of who you are and the value of your life and your love was declared by God when He created you and said, "Ooh, she's good, fearfully and wonderfully made." Believe it. Act as if you believe it, and others will too. Don't put yourself on sale. You are a designer original. Everyone cannot afford the price you demand and that's all right. If they could, you would be common, and God designed you to be unique and set apart. Who told you those awful things about yourself? You'd better rehearse what God says about you and settle the matter in your heart once and for all. Otherwise you will settle for one small bite of fruit when you could be partaking of a whole garden.

A Fair Deal

Then He (Jesus) said, "Beware of all covetousness, a man's life
does not consist in the abundance of his possessions."

LUKE 12:15 RSV

You can only covet what you do not have. The more you
focus on the lack of love in your life, the larger and
more overwhelming your desire becomes. It becomes
an idol, demanding more of your thoughts and energy than it
ever should. You become convinced that life is not full until you
have what you feel you need to make yourself complete. This is
the subtlety of the lie. Let's face it, you are still living whether
you have the love you want or not. Life consists of only what
we do with it. So, get on with it.

Only you can shuffle the cards that you have been dealt.
Play the game and play to win. Don't weep over not having the
perfect deck. Someone needs something that is in your hand.
Life is interactive. As we learn to share what we've been given,
we eventually get all we need. The progression of living day-to-
day eventually evens the score if we play long enough.

Peeking at someone else's hand can get us in trouble. Coveting their cards can get us in bigger trouble. After all, you don't
know what else comes with their deck and the price they will
have to pay for it. Simply trust that the Master Dealer has dis-
tributed the cards according to what He knew you could handle
right now. If every good and perfect gift comes from above, you
must believe that if what you desired was good and perfect for

your life right now, God would make sure that you had it. He says He will withhold no good thing from you. Therefore, believe that His timing is perfect and that when the desires of your heart are perfected He will graciously present them to you. Until then, don't believe the hype or get caught up in having eyes that are wandering where they don't belong. What looks good to you isn't always good *for* you. Oh, but when it is, it will be yours for the asking.

Ticktock

"Sing, O barren woman, you who never bore a child; burst into song, shout for joy, you who were never in labour; because more are the children of the desolate woman than of her who has a husband," says the Lord.

ISAIAH 54:1 NLT

elp! My biological clock is ticking! Doesn't God know I'm running out of time?!" Well, I've settled this issue. My clock is broken. It no longer clangs in my ears. We can set a clock on the mantel of our hearts and work ourselves into a fine frenzy if we insist on staring at it. Or, we can search for other ways to be fruitful. In God's economy, He uses those who have an unusual surplus to minister to the needy. Could it be that God wants you to birth babies in another way? To have spiritual children? If everything begins in the spirit before manifesting in the natural, perhaps the tack to take is this: I will be a mother to the motherless.

Consider your options. First there are children crying out for love and attention all around us. Some have parents who are simply too busy. Some have no parents. Then there are those who are waiting to be born in spirit. Through your prayers, influence, and encouragement, they can be birthed into the kingdom. Spiritual babies that you can nurture into the fullness of spiritual maturity. The rewards for raising up people in the ways of the Lord are priceless.

God wants us to be filled with purpose. This is also what our soul craves most. Many women who become mothers ask themselves the same question as their lives become filled with raising someone who is totally dependent on them in their early years. "What is my purpose? Is this all I'm living for?" Their lives become consumed by their children and their sense of identity suffers. They long for more to live for—like adult conversation and a vision beyond diapers. God finds value in both natural motherhood and spiritual motherhood. Is your biological clock ticking? Then become fruitful right where you are.

Empty Calories

*When you are full, you will refuse honey, but when you are
hungry, even bitter food tastes sweet.*

PROVERBS 27:7 TEV

Ever notice that when you're hungry everything looks
good? I always suggest that you should never go to a
restaurant when you are starving. Everything on the
menu seems appealing, including stuff you wouldn't normally
like. But after you've ordered and taken a few bites, the edge is
off your hunger and the truth sinks in. You will never be able
to eat it all. You don't even want it. It doesn't taste as good as it
sounded on the menu! Why? Because you were being driven by
your appetite.

Our soul should be well satisfied in every aspect of life so
that we make discerning choices on what we allow into our
hearts. Otherwise, we find ourselves hungry for love and looking for it in all the wrong places. Whether it's obsessions with
food, material possessions, accomplishments, or just bad men,
the root is the same—hunger. Hunger for a natural desire that
God has placed in our hearts. However, because we have failed
to eat what He has given us, we find ourselves starving for attention and doing all the wrong things to get it. Small wonder
He tells us to stop filling up on things that will never be able to
satisfy us.

Be spiritually full. Have a full life. Be satisfied from the
inside out. When Satan comes offering you tasty fast food—

unsaved men, premarital sex, inappropriate fondling, food, too many sweets, overindulgence of every sort, the wrong types of entertainment, compensatory addictions, like shopping...you name it, whatever it is he's offering to sedate your senses—don't settle for his deceptive menu. He knows that if you partake of enough of them, you will be open for anything. No, my sister, you've come too far and waited too long to fill up on empty calories. You know the type. They taste good going down, but they don't digest well, and they are fattening. In short they don't do anything good for your body or your soul. No, no, no. Push them away and hold out for the main course.

Craving Control

If you do well, you are accepted; if not, sin is a
demon crouching at the door. It shall be eager for you,
and you will be mastered by it.

GENESIS 4:7 NEB

So if the Lord isn't going to give me what I want right now, why doesn't He just take the desire away? I hear that, but let me set you free. It's not going to happen. God is not going to just lift the desire for a man, physical intimacy, chocolate, whatever it is that we're craving out of our systems. He wants us to be masters over our desires. He gave us those desires; we have just let them run amuck! You see, He has already given us everything we need in order to fulfill our calling in life and live in a godly fashion. Therefore, He expects us to use our spiritual muscles to get around the track of life.

Is your desire for love in your life a sin? Absolutely not! However, if it has become an idol—if it consumes all your thoughts 24/7 and affects every decision you make—then I would dare to say you've crossed the line. You are on dangerous ground. What you are really saying is that God is not enough. Not enough to satisfy you. That true fulfillment can be found apart from Him. This was the original sin.

When Eve sinned, God took it as rejection. She wanted something more than Him. She sought fulfillment apart from Him. So He let her have the independence she wanted, but, oh, what she lost! Part of the consequence of her new-found independence was that her desire for her man to validate and fulfill her would rule over her. She would be in bondage to her need for Adam. She didn't realize that when she disconnected herself from God she also disconnected herself from Adam. God, unbeknownst to her, was the thing that made them one. He was the third cord that bound them together securely. But she severed the cord and found herself feeling very cold and lonely in the draft of her new-found freedom.

Anytime we choose to find satisfaction independent from God, we find ourselves suffering the same consequences. God, who has given us everything, is a jealous lover. When we cling to something other than Him to complete us, because God created us with a free will, He will allow that desire to consume us to the point where we finally realize that what we're clinging to will never take the place, that only He can fill in our hearts. Yet while we pursue other lovers, God is watching and waiting the whole time, jealous for our attention. And fortunately, when we wake up to our error, He will draw us back with His loving-kindness, showing us that no one is capable of loving us as much as He does.

Will He take your desire for love and affection and attention away? No, because He wants us to desire those things from Him. It's when our focus shifts south of heaven that our desires get the best of us. So let's rein in those desires and put them in the right perspective. Remember, you should have desires, but they should not have you.

Timing Is Everything

*To everything there is a season, a time for every
purpose under heaven.*

ECCLESIASTES 3:1 NKJV

That would include a time to be single and a time to be married. Every smart woman knows that timing is everything. A word spoken too soon can be a deal breaker. Hold your peace and let the chips fall where they may. But you have to trust the One who holds the chips in order to be able to do that. More importantly, in the scheme of life, God has numbered our days, our times, and the purposes of our seasons. Trust Him. He knows what He's doing.

Throw out all of the questions and speculations. No, nothing is wrong with you. You don't need to lose weight, gain weight, cut your hair, or do anything different. At least not for the sake of getting a man. Now if it's about you working on being a better you, then all right. No, you're not being too picky. If God has promised to surpass your imagination with the gifts He has for you, then what's the problem? What I'm saying, bottom line, is this—we could all work on improving ourselves. However, the motivation should not be to win the attention and validation of a man. In most cases, we are where we are simply because of God's timing and divine plan for our lives.

This is why it is so important for us to know what we're supposed to be doing with ourselves in the meantime. We should be taking advantage of where we are and redeeming our time as singles to the utmost. The time is coming when you will have different priorities and not as much time to do as you please should you marry. Therefore, seize the season at hand and live in it to the fullest.

Single Solitude

In the same way, a woman who is no longer married or has never been married can be more devoted to the Lord in body and in spirit, while the married woman must be concerned about her earthly responsibilities and how to please her husband.

1 CORINTHIANS 7:34 NLT

Hey, let's face it, men are distracting! Marriage takes time and work if you're going to do it right. The energy required to coordinate schedules, deal with children, do domestic chores, and still find time for romance can be a full-time job. Marriage and having a relationship with God both do the same thing. They change your life. They take over. They hold you accountable for your decisions and the way you spend your time.

I'm always fascinated when I hear my married women friends bemoaning the fact that they have to struggle to fit in their quiet time with God. This seems to be one of the things they miss most from their single life. Now they have to be up and at 'em preparing the day for their husbands and children. Moments of solitude are rare.

Oh, the things we take for granted as single women! I know that my own life would have to change if I had a husband. It would have to slow *waaaaay* down. Perhaps a part of me keeps as busy as I do to distract myself from the fact that no one is there. In all honesty, my philosophy is: Why stay at home if I don't have to? However, there has to be a balance between living it up and putting life on hold. That balance is found in focusing on the purpose God has for your life. Discerning if every activity is a good idea or a God idea. Remember, if Satan can't beat you, he will join you. He will fill your life with so much activity you just wear yourself right on out. What happens when you wear yourself out? You get depressed. This is when the serpent whispers, "See, you've given your all for God and He still hasn't given you what you want. How fair is that?"

Don't go there. Don't have that conversation. It leads to nowhere except being unable to love the life you are living. The truth of the matter is that God has a purpose for you. As you get busy in your purpose, it will lead you to the place where your desires await you. You can't miss them because if they are behind you, they will overtake you. If they are in front of you, they will wait for you. God appreciates your labor. He has taken note of every seed sown, so don't get weary of well-doing. In the right season, you will reap all that your heart longs for and more. In hindsight, you will be able to understand the plan, even though you can't see the fine details right now. Wait on the Lord. That's a double entendre. Wait as in wait. And wait as in serve Him. Take advantage of the opportunity to concentrate on what is at hand. The rest will come, and it will be "all good."

Soon Enough

*Nevertheless, each one should retain
the place in life that the Lord assigned to
him and to which God has called him.*

1 CORINTHIANS 7:17

Where are you right now? Take stock of your life. So you are single. For now that is God's assigned season for your life. Live in the moment and make the best of it. Seasons do change. Wearing summer clothes in the middle of winter has never made summer come any sooner. Therefore deal with where you are joyfully. Find out what God would have you do to occupy your time, talents, and energy this day, this week, and try not to look any further. Jesus said to concentrate on today for tomorrow and its troubles would come soon enough. I can testify to that!

There will never be a time like right now in your life to do all that you have ever longed to do. To accomplish whatever goals you have set for yourself. And yes, you *should* have goals. A woman without a vision for her life will perish sure as she's born. God did not create you to simply exist. He fashioned you with something to do in mind. Find out what it is and get busy. Begin with where you are. Be faithful with the little things. Would you or your abode look different if you were married? Then get busy fixing. When you're ready, he will come. And if he delays, you will still be living up to your full potential, which always releases a flood of joy and a sense of great accomplishment. Go ahead, get on with the business of living the immediate life with all that is within you. Be all that you can be now. The rest will come soon enough.

Stick to the Script

*My purpose is to do the will of my Father
and to finish His work...*

JOHN 4:34 NLT

First things first. Let's put our priorities in order before we talk about love and men. We were created for God. Created to be worshipers. Created as a mate for His Son Jesus. None of us are here by chance. You are here *on* purpose with a divine purpose to complete. God had something in mind when He formed you in your mother's womb. Before you were conceived He knew you. Is that deep or what?

Our lives are like a movie. First there was the screenplay. God had a vision of how everything would go. Then He cast you in the leading role. Remember, the role existed before you filled it. Now when you started reading the script, you ran into conflict. But God was not surprised by the twists and turns in the plot because He already knew about them. He also knows the end of the story. He doesn't allow anyone to rewrite the story. He wants us to stick to the script. When we do, the perfect design of our purpose becomes clear and the story has a happy ending. Maybe the boy gets the girl and they live happily ever after, or the girl simply gets a fabulous life and lives happily ever after.

The script that God has written for your life is one of eternal love and fulfillment. But this will only take place if you follow His direction. Yes, He is the director of the movie, too. If you allow

Him to edit out the bad scenes and splice together the parts that are pleasing to Him, a beautiful story will unfold. Award-winning stuff. The type of story that will fulfill His purposes and bring Him glory. And what do you get out of the deal? Joy, power, peace, and a whole lot of exciting scenes and surprising sequels far beyond what you've ever imagined.

Personal Enrichment

Jesus said…"I have come so that you can have life and have it more abundantly."

JOHN 10:7,10

Do you feel as if you are living life to the fullest right now? Or are you running on "E"? Half-full with the meter going up and down according to your various circumstances? It's time to pull over and assess your situation. Life is meant to be lived to the fullest according to God. You should be charging through it with gusto! You've heard the saying, "Dance as if no one is watching." Fling your hands in the air and go for it. Do something you've never done. Go somewhere you've never gone before. Meet someone new. Have something to talk about. Besides Jesus.

Now don't get excited. Hear me out. Jesus should be such an integrated part of your life that it is like living and breathing Him. So He is the one big given. But remember, Jesus was very well versed on all types of other topics. That's why He was able to break the Gospel down to a level everyone could understand. He related to them where they lived. Don't be so heavenly minded that you are of no earthly good. Be knowledgeable about the Word, but stimulate the interests of acquaintances by having other areas of conversation that are intriguing. You should be able to marry natural experiences to heavenly truths. In other words, your relationship with the Lord should be in the natural flow of things, not a forced issue. That's the difference between relationship and religion.

If you feel bored, it's your fault. It's time to tap into your imagination and come up with a dream. Then weave it. It might be something as simple as learning needlepoint, but watch what begins to happen. One new thing unlocks another new thing and soon your life is filled with interesting things that put a light in your eyes that others are attracted to.

How does one live the abundant life? By trying out all of your various options. And believe me, my friend, there's more to life than church and work. God has created all things beautiful. Get out there and enjoy them.

The Facts of Life....

Tomorrow is not promised; therefore, squeeze every bit of enjoyment out of today.

Life is a superb banquet. Savor every bite, digest it slowly, but never bite off more than you can chew.

Life is what you make it. Others can only add to what you have prepared.

If you are bored with life, you will be boring to whomever you would find interesting. Don't just be interested, be interesting.

You get what you give; therefore, give love and plenty of it.

Life is not a juggling act. It is to be carefully balanced and carried with grace.

The greatest story ever told will be about your life. What would you like others to read or see? Decide and then follow the script.

Inner Glow

Well done, good and faithful servant; you were faithful over a few things, I will make you ruler over many things. Enter into the joy of your lord.

MATTHEW 25:21 NKJV

*I*t is not what you are looking forward to that is important. It is where you are right now that matters the most. What are you doing with your life at this present moment? Are you being a good steward over all that the Lord is presently providing? Are you being a wise steward of your money? What about the place where you live? Have you made it a home or does it still look like a temporary dwelling place? Are you honing all your skills as a woman? Can you cook? If a potential mate asked you to fill out a resumé, would your abilities and achievements qualify for the awesome job of being a wife? If not, get busy, sister!

Remember that while you are getting blessed by the man in your life you are also to be a blessing to him. You are to be the "good thing" that he finds. Occupy your time until the man comes, and be ready. Prepare yourself now. Practice the fine art of homemaking. Decorate. Set your house in order. Learn to prepare simple, tasty meals. Work up a repertoire that he can select from. Develop yourself as a woman. You don't have to be a size two, but you should be fit. If you feel good, you will look good. If you look good, you will be attractive to others.

Being faithful over what you can control in your world right now sets you up to gain more than you ever imagined. However, if your stuff isn't together, why would God add to what you already cannot handle? Come on now, think about it. Can He trust you with more if what you already have overwhelms you? This does not have to be exasperating. Start with where you are. Take stock of your personal world and note what is needed, what is missing, or what can stand to be improved. Write out a list of things to do and begin to do them one at a time. This could be anything from painting a room to getting a new career, but the results will be the same. An extraordinary thing will happen. You will find a sense of accomplishment rising on the inside of you that will produce great joy in your inner woman. All of a sudden you will have a fabulous glow that others will notice. That is the joy of the Lord. A sense of well-being from knowing that everything is well with you. That you are walking in divine purpose and all is in order. That you are doing your best with the life you've been served. Once you get started, it can only get better.

Welcome to His Place, a seven-star restaurant with the finest dining on the planet. Sit back, relax, enjoy the experience, and allow Him to serve you.

The Menu of Life

APPETIZERS

Promise Promenade—A tantalizing sampler of God's promises for your life. Promises of good and perfect gifts to give you a future and a hope. One bite will prepare your palate for tasty delights to follow.

Serendipity Salad—A fresh medley of God's goodness mingled with wonderful surprises in every bite. Chance meetings and refreshing encounters ordered up by our stellar Chef that will come back to your remembrance in the days to come. This dish could be addictive!

Clear Consommé—Light, spicy, and warming within. It is said that it makes one's vision clearer. Satisfying and surprisingly purposeful, it prepares your palate for any other dish you select.

Cool, Cold, Chillin' Soup—Each sip will bring refreshment as you have never tasted. Light, flavorful, restful, and nutritious. This does a body and spirit good. A breath of fresh air that revives you to face the world.

Dreamweaver's Cocktail—Spicy bites of overwhelming possibilities to put a spark in your eye and a lilt in your step. A little filling, but will always leave room for the main course.

ENTRÉES

Grilled Lamb—A tender and succulent offering. Pricey, but worth every bite. Hand selected, only the finest. You won't taste anything better. This dish will stay with you and flavor your life.

Savory Sautéed Manna—God's directions for your life served up warm and fresh in an aromatic stew that is sure to make your mouth water. Each bite is better than the last. Pungent, stick-to-your ribs fare that will fill you and strengthen you for the journey.

Stir-Fried Surprise—No bite is the same, though the flavor is consistent throughout. One of our most exciting dishes. Served over a bed of yielded rice and sprinkled with fragrant oils that stimulate a zest for life. Oh-so-tasty, this dish is full of promise.

El Shaddai's Stacked Sandwich—This is the feast of life! Seemingly never ending. Fresh grace, goodness, and mercy in every bite. This one satisfies your deepest longings and fills every empty space in your being. Fortifies you with strength, vitality, and an overall sense of well-being. A hefty serving but good to the last crumb. Topped with the Chef's secret sauce.

DESSERT

Passionfruit Sorbet—For the romantic in you. Smooth and light but with substance. It goes down easy, leaving a haunting taste you can savor. Downright delicious. This treat will have you smiling like the cat who just ate the canary.

Jubilee Cake—Every bite will fill your mouth with joy and your tongue with laughter. It's a recipe that everyone will want to taste. Bubbly, delectable, but not fattening, this one is good for the soul.

Goody Goody Pie—Delight that isn't detrimental to your system. The perfect end to a filling meal. Topped with a healthy serving of blessed sauce.

Heavenly Hash—A house favorite. Combines all the goodness of the Chef's special stash in a creative mix that's sure to stimulate your sense of adventure for the finer things in life. Indescribable, you just have to taste it to believe it.

BEVERAGES

Living Waters—Purified waters flown in fresh from a special fountain reserved for the house. One sip and you will never thirst again. Served still or sparkling.

Comfort Tea—For restless souls. Has been compared to chamomile but with more lasting results. Served at just the right temperature in a special vessel to preserve its healing qualities.

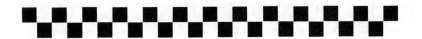

Fruit Punch—Truly unique in flavor. Every sip is a spiritual experience. Rich in consistency, bold in its taste, yet with a gentle bouquet. Everyone will want a refill.

SIDE DISHES

Candied Medley—Brain food. Said to increase perception, wisdom, and understanding. Delicious. The more you taste, the more you want.

Souffléd Grains—Will improve your sense of well-being and give you stamina. The perfect side for those who have a hunger for life.

Sautéed Delight—This dish has a wealth of bounty. All the best from the Chef's cupboard goes into this incredible medley to create a dish that others will envy you for. Eat, enjoy, and share. There's plenty to go around.

Roasted Favor—You will have everyone's interest when you order this one. It sets the stage for whatever else you choose from the menu. This one prepares your palate for all the other dishes. It's a must-taste. Truly good.

* When in doubt on menu choices, ask the Holy Spirit what the Chef recommends.

BON APPÉTIT!

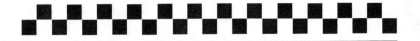

Love...

¹sing \'siŋ\ vb sang \'saŋ\ or sung \'səŋ\; sung; sing·ing \'siŋ-iŋ\ [ME singen, fr. OE singan; akin to OHG singan to sing, Gk omphē voice] vi (bef. 12c) **1 a** : to produce musical tones by means of the voice **b** : to utter words in musical tones and with musical inflections and modulations **c** : to deliver songs as a trained or professional singer **2** : to make a shrill whining or whistling sound **3 a** : to relate or celebrate something in verse **b** : to compose poetry **4** : to produce musical or harmonious sounds **5** : BUZZ, RING **6** : to make a cry : CALL **7** : to give information or evidence ~ vt **1** : to utter with musical inflections; esp : to interpret in musical tones produced by the voice **2** : to relate or celebrate in verse **3** : CHANT, INTONE **4** : to bring or accompany to a place or state by singing ⟨~s the child to sleep⟩ — sing·able \'siŋ-ə-bəl\ adj

Single /ˈsiŋ-gəl/ adj **1a:** not married **b:** of or relating to celibacy **2:** unaccompanied by others: LONE, SOLE **3a:** (1) consisting of or having only one part, feature, or portion (2) consisting of one as opposed to or in contrast with many (3) consisting of only one in number **4a:** consisting of a separate unique whole **5b:** exclusively attentive **6:** unbroken, undivided **7:** having no equal or like: SINGULAR **8:** designed for the use of one person only.

Single n **1a:** a separate individual person or thing **b:** an unmarried person.

Single vb **1:** to select or distinguish from a number or group. **2a:** to advance or score.

sin·gle–cell protein \,siŋ-gəl-,sel-\ n (ca. 1967) : protein produced by microorganisms cultured on organic material and used esp. as a source of food
single combat n (1610) : combat between two persons
single cross n (1940) : a first-generation hybrid between two selected and usu. inbred lines — compare DOUBLE CROSS
single entry n (1826) : a method of bookkeeping that recognizes only one side of a business transaction and usu. consists only of a record of cash and personal accounts with debtors and creditors

Wait a Minute...

*B*efore we can go any further with this conversation about love, we need to get clear on some things. Before you begin to pursue love, you need to know what it is you are getting yourself into. Perhaps you will slow down, perhaps you will run even faster, but I owe you all the facts so that you can make a quality choice.

Before you can love anyone else, your love for God and yourself must be intact. So let's get the order right. God first, you second, everyone else after that. If these areas are not addressed, it can only lead to unhappy love exchanges that never give you the fulfillment you want or rightfully expect. Yes, the act of receiving true love begins with you. And this whole love thing is really between you and God. If you can't get it right with Him, the One who created love and is love personified, then who *can* you get it right with? Yes, the romance must begin before a man ever enters your life. Remember, love attracts more love. *So how do I get there, Michelle?* Hold on, I'm about to tell you how to get the love you want step-by-step. And you'll find joy along the way while you wait for Mr. Right.

Love is not about what you can get.
It's about what you give.
Therefore love is always available…
If you truly want it.

The Gift of Giving

God so loved the world that he gave...

JOHN 3:16

*P*erhaps in your pursuit for it you saw love as the end-all-be-all answer to your heart's desires. In truth, it will be the greatest test of your willingness to sacrifice. "But I thought I was supposed to be getting something out of love!" you say. "I thought it was supposed to make me feel good. Make me feel validated and fulfilled and important because someone wants me." Hmm, that's not exactly what God had in mind. If we are to follow God's perfect model of love, we must be of the mind-set to give more than we receive. After all, it is more blessed to do so. The purest delight of love is pouring out all that you have on one who recognizes the worth of your offerings, but that might not always be the case. Give anyway. God did.

Jesus looked forward to the time when we would recognize and return His love. He gave much more than we will ever be able to return. Even so, it gave Him pleasure to know that His sacrifice would change our lives and destinies forever. When you give love to someone, they will never be the same because of you. Love is deep, profound, and life-changing. Not everyone has the capacity or the ability to respond to it adeptly, yet it never fails to affect all that it touches. For some, the effect of love is more immediate. For others, it reshapes their hearts. You will never know the full effect of your love in the lives of some.

Years later, the recipient will pause to remember a word you spoke, a gesture you offered, and ponder its effect on their lives. Love is everlasting.

So think about your motivation for reaching out to those you strive to attract. Is it because of what you long to give to them? Or is it because of what you believe they will add to your life? Do you already have what you are seeking from them? Your answer should be yes. Only God can fill you with that which you long to receive from others. Then you can give back to them. Such is the cycle of true love, to give and give again. It is in the giving that you get what you are looking for.

God gave His son to gain us for His own. There will never be a dearer sacrifice. If we are called to be like Him, we must imitate even this—to lay down our selfish motives of grasping at the hearts of others.

Contrary to popular belief

love is not the answer to all our problems

In truth it may be the catalyst to many

so immense can be the pain of sacrifice

which walks hand in hand with love

However,

love is not synonymous with pain

selfishness is…

For your soul longs to imitate Christ

in acts of selflessness

Give

lest you disappoint it…

Sold Out

*Love the Lord your God with all your heart, and with
all your soul, and with all your mind, and with all your strength.*

MARK 12:30 NASB

Some ask the question, "Why does God want so much of us? Isn't He being selfish?" The answer to that is: Not at all. He just wants what is due Him. If you created something, breathed the breath of life into it, nurtured it, and provided for its every need, wouldn't you want your creation to love you more than life itself? Nothing wounds a parent like a disrespectful, unappreciative child.

This brings us back full circle to our original thought. If we love the Lord as we should, our hearts will bask in His protective care. We will be much more discerning about our love choices and avoid a lot of heartbreak. God Himself ordained marriage and wants to deliver you to the arms of another. But only to the man who He knows will love you the way He does. He won't trust just anyone with your heart. So why should you?

Lavishing our love on the One who loves us most keeps us in a position of safety as well as fullness of joy. As we pour out our love on Him, our first fiancé, we will become well-kept women. After all, loving someone with all your heart, soul, mind, and strength will take up a lot of time and energy. You've got to put everything into it. Be sold out completely to loving and living inside of that love.

Is your love for God merely intellectual? It's not enough because we change our minds constantly based on circumstances. Is your love for God only emotional? This, too, is not enough. You must have a reason, a basis for your love. Is your love for God something you pursue with due diligence, with every fiber of your being through endless works of righteousness that sap you of your strength at times? Hmm, this is dangerous alone. Going through the motions of loving God will soon replace a joyous relationship with sour-faced religiosity. Is your love for God merely soulish? If so, you will constantly be at war with your flesh as you fluctuate over what you love most. Many things appeal to our soul, but it is difficult to love them all equally at the same time. Something will suffer.

We've got to have a made-up mind to give our hearts completely to God, ordering our soul to resist the urges of the flesh with all of our strength. Our capacity to give and receive love from others depends on it.

Pouring Out

Love your neighbor as yourself.

LUKE 10:27

*O*ops! There it is! If you are commanded to love your neighbor as you love yourself, then that means you have got to love yourself. Not in a New Age, humanistic sort of way, but God's way. What do you do with something that you love? You take good care of it. Revere it. Understand its worth and treat it accordingly. You pamper it. You make sure it always looks its best. You don't do anything to harm it or put it in harm's way. Uh-huh, we're talking about you, girl.

Do you treat others the same? Think about it. If you are always putting yourself down, you are most likely being very critical of others as well. You see, God understood that you could only treat the next person as well as you treat yourself. If you have a good, healthy opinion of yourself, you will be able to celebrate the strengths of others. However, if you don't like yourself, it's hard to celebrate when others around you look well and do well. This will only heighten your disappointment with yourself. It becomes a vicious cycle that is hard to break. Take a tip from me. Lighten up. Don't take yourself so seriously. Learn to laugh at your mistakes. Consider your quirks a stroke of God's genius that makes you unique rather than something negative. Learn to see your life as half-full instead of half-empty. Don't turn away a compliment—embrace it and internalize it. Use it as a guidepost to get more.

For many years I struggled with my weight. I would look in the mirror and criticize my body. I would starve it. Talk sternly to it and tell it to line up. I found myself growing larger. One day the Lord spoke to me and said, "Michelle, be kind to your body. It's the only one you have. Love it and it will serve you." So I began looking at myself in a different way. I started noting the good parts of me. I began to celebrate my body. I took it for regular massages. Selected good foods for it. I began to listen to my body. It had been reacting badly to many of the things I was putting into my system. I no longer forced these things on my body. I ate what it craved in moderation. I took it for walks. Began to seek clothing that complemented its good points. Guess what? I began to lose weight! I started to feel better and look better. I loved my body and my body was loving me back. Are you going where I'm taking you? To a land of celebration.

If you can train yourself to respond to yourself with kindness, it will naturally overflow to others. When you love yourself, you won't be as self-conscious. You will be free in spirit to look beyond yourself and respond to the needs of others wholeheartedly. As you begin to pour out sensitivity and responsiveness to others around you, fulfillment and joy will flood your being. You will rejoice in the positive and find grace for the negative. Remember, what a woman sows is definitely what she will reap. Therefore, sow love.

A True Love Connection

*Your attitude should be the same as that of Christ Jesus: Who,
being in very nature God, did not consider equality with God
something to be grasped, but made himself nothing, taking the very
nature of a servant, being made in human likeness. And being
found in appearance as a man, he humbled himself and became
obedient to death—even death on a cross! Therefore God exalted
him to the highest place and gave him the name that is above every
name, that at the name of Jesus every knee should bow, in heaven
and on earth and under the earth, and every tongue confess that
Jesus Christ is Lord, to the glory of God the Father.*

PHILIPPIANS 2:5-11

To think that one person would do all of that for a relationship is astounding. The only way you can humble yourself to the extent Jesus did (in order to clear the way for us to have a romance with Him throughout eternity) is to know and love yourself and know your personal worth first. Consider the analogy of bungee jumping, if you will. No bungee jumpers are going anywhere until they know the line that keeps them from crashing is secure. They know that although they are flinging themselves out into the open air, descending from the highest heights to the lowest lows, they are connected and guaranteed a safe return.

When we are truly experiencing a love connection with God, secure within ourselves that we are lovable, we are able to take risks to love others—without expecting anything in return.

Unconditional love. There is something so freeing about not re-
lying on anyone's love to validate you! You've already got all the
love you need. Anything else from others is merely icing on the
cake of your heart. You are not empty. Not starving. Not in desperate need. Therefore, you make choices to give love to those
around you without requiring anything in return. Of course, this
is the secret to getting the love you want. Your openhandedness
frees others to make the choice to love you back. Unconditional
release attracts ardent commitment, but conditional neediness
smothers the promise of love. It snuffs the life and joy out of love
because others are being robbed of the their power to choose. So
stay connected to the love vine and freely give its fruit. Freely give
and freely receive.

On Guard!

Guard your heart more than any treasure,
for it is the source of all life.

PROVERBS 4:23 NEB

*I*f you love yourself, you will protect what is dear. That would be your heart. Your heart condition affects everything concerning your life. Guard it as in care for, preserve, keep out of harm's way, nurture. Though the heart must take risks when it comes to love, those risks should be thought out, not impulsively executed. Consider the cost but also consider the rewards. Observe the fine line but don't allow it to trip you. The heart is the seat of decision making in your being. Therefore, consider your offerings before you give them, measure them into servings that don't overwhelm or deplete. Give of yourself as an offering to God, not in search of something in return. Dare to love, to give, to serve, to empty yourself as Christ did for you.

So how does one guard the heart and take risks at the same time? Consider one who is in a fencing match. "On guard!" they proclaim. Yet their arms are open as they do their dance back and forth jabbing, stepping away from the tip of the other's sword. How do they guard their hearts? By wearing the right protection. Their chests are secure behind a shield. You see, they don't stand with their hands over their hearts protecting them. That would hinder movement. They move freely, trusting their armor to protect what is vital. We too have armor, the armor of God. God has promised to keep what is committed to Him; therefore, give Him your heart. Ask Him to hold it and then dare to dance.

Build a fence around your heart

not a wall.

Allow others to see

but not readily touch.

Let them approach

and behold,

To consider its beauty

and decide if they can

answer its invitation...

Should they walk away,

remember the value of the property

has not decreased...

Dare to Desire

The heart is deceitful above all things and beyond cure.
Who can understand it?

JEREMIAH 17:9

And he who searches our hearts knows the mind of the Spirit, be-
cause the Spirit intercedes for the saints in accordance with God's
will. And we know that in all things God works for the good of
those who love him, who have been called according to his purpose.

ROMANS 8:27-28

*I*n our former life before Christ, our hearts were at war with God. We wanted things He did not want for us, we could not trust our hearts or even what we chose to love. But now we are in Christ. Our hearts are in tune with His heart. Our desires are in harmony with His if we are walking uprightly before Him. Make friends with your heart. Listen to it. It is the instrument that God uses to give us direction. Some of those desires might cause us to be fearful. Is this what God really wants for me? I don't dare long for such a thing!

I recall wanting a car. I had very specific desires. I wanted a good car. In my heart of hearts I really wanted a nice car, but my mind convinced me to settle for something that was capable and not expensive. However, in the end through a divine connection, I ended up getting an older Mercedes for an amazingly low price. It was actually cheaper than the economy cars I had been considering. I felt as if this one incident was God's way of saying, "Do not be afraid to want what you want. I am willing to give it to you if you will only acknowledge what you want and release it back to Me." Now that Mercedes is not what I would have initially chosen. But the moment I took one ride in it, I was in love. Since then, it has served me well, and I didn't have to enter into debt to possess it. God took the heart of my desire, mingled it with what He knew was best for me, and delivered a blessing above my imagination.

Don't be afraid to dream, to hope, to desire what you want. Trust that God is guiding your heart. If you are going down the wrong avenue, the Holy Spirit will intercede for you and God will place a detour in your path to redirect you. Make sure you are willing to yield to the change of direction. Let go and let God. Follow the yellow brick road and see where it leads. If you are walking hand in hand with Him, though you may venture through a murky forest, you will find your way back home. Home to a blessing that will make you rich in love, rich in experience, and rich in the knowledge of God's goodness and keeping power. Yes, it will make you rich and add no sorrow.

Just Friends

There is no fear in love. But perfect love drives out fear, because
fear has to do with punishment. The one who fears is not made
perfect in love. We love because he first loved us.

1 JOHN 4:18-19

I have a friend whom I adore. He is just a friend. I could be
interested. But he is not. Yet we have a very rich friendship that I would have missed out on if I had decided that
I would not share my heart with him because his desire toward
me was not the same. Recently he told me about a woman who
he was interested in. I said, "I'm jealous!" He said, "You can't be
jealous. You should want me to be happy." My reply was, "Yes, I
can. It's a healthy feeling that I am sharing with you, and yes, I
do want you to be happy." To which he said, "Oh I get it, you
want me to be happy, just as long as I'm alone!" "Yes, that's it!"
I laughed. And we both had a big chuckle over it. I did not walk
away hurt because he had not chosen me. I know that he loves
me in a different way, and I did not feel rejected. I knew that I
still had the best part of what I needed from him. An incredible
friendship that would be lasting because of our honesty and
lack of expectations from one another.

How could I be so calm about this scenario? Because I already feel loved. I am not fearful of sharing my heart with others because it is already complete in Christ. I sense and feel His
love and protection in my life every single day. I feel Him thinking about me. I notice every surprise that He plans for me. I see

His kindness and assistance extended to me through others, and I don't take one nicety for granted. When it is settled that we are already getting all the love we deserve, we will be more loving to others and thus get a bountiful measure of love and caring returned to us.

I must confess that I used to expect the worst from every man I met. Somewhere in my subconscious I must have felt that I deserved their lack of interest and mistreatment. The problem was not them. It was me. I lived in fear of punishment. Somewhere along the way I had believed the lie that I was unlovable. God has proven to me that this is not true, having been made perfect in His love. I now can be mature in my expectations of others and be realistic about what they are capable of giving. I no longer pursue relationships with others who are not able to give me what I need. I am able to love because the Lover of my soul has loved me first. It is a joyous place full of rich relationships that I might have overlooked before.

Have you insisted that every man you meet fit into the mold of your expectations? If you are wondering why there are no men in your life, the answer to this question is probably yes. If you're ready to start experiencing pleasant surprises and a happier life, it's time to gain balance and stretch beyond your comfort zone. To accept the love you have and cause it to increase by giving it away generously. Plant love and reap it in return. Just make sure you are planting it in good ground.

The Scent of Love

Pleasing is the fragrance of your perfumes.
SONG OF SONGS 1:3

I believe there is a pheromone that is released in your system when you are in love. When you feel loved there is a glow on your countenance that no amount of makeup can imitate. It's like a magnet drawing the attention of others. They sense the joy and it is irresistible. In the Song of Solomon when the Shulammite woman proudly proclaimed, "I am my Beloved's, his desire is for me and his banner over me is love!" everyone applauded her beauty and her desirability. We must walk in love before we can attract love.

I recall going shopping with some friends one day. I was looking at a display case that we had all perused with nothing catching anyone's eye. All of a sudden I spotted an article that I thought was absolutely beautiful. As I *oohed* and *aahed* over it, my friends began to also admire the piece, which I had now decided to purchase. "How could we have overlooked that!" they exclaimed. Now this overlooked article had suddenly become the desire of everyone. I became the proud owner because I had recognized its beauty and worth first.

God has recognized your beauty and worth first. He first loved you. As you receive and bask in His love and admiration, others will have to line up with His opinion of you. Which, by the way, will always be greater than your opinion of yourself because He is looking at you through the blood of Jesus, which covers all of your flaws.

As you surround yourself with the aroma of His love, which emanates from the fruit of the Spirit being at work in your life (you know, all of that good stuff like goodness, kindness, patience), others will admire your fragrance and draw closer to enjoy its bouquet. "What is that incredible scent you're wearing?" they will ask. "Ah, that would be Eau de Love," you will reply with a fabulous smile.

A Hearing Heart

I love the Lord, for he heard my voice;
he heard my cry for mercy.

PSALM 116:1

*L*et's examine why we love who we love. We love them because we feel heard and understood by them. We love them because we feel they have tapped into our hearts and made a connection with us. They respond to our heart's cry and fill a need. This makes us feel loved and we love them in return.

So if this is what it takes for us to love someone, it would stand to reason that if we want love, we should have listening hearts that respond to the needs of others. Here we are back to giving again. It doesn't seem as if we can get away from it. But in today's "what have you done for me lately" society, it becomes easier to be a grasper instead of a giver. After all, every one of us has our own personal fires to put out, right? Most conversations are rather one-sided if we examine them. With no thought to the other person, we ask people, "How are you?" But do we really hear? Many a "fine" response is tinged with pain or frustration but not taken note of. These people walk away feeling disconnected from us. We wonder why we don't hear from them anymore when they seemed to be so interested before...

The truth of the matter is we are all made to depend on one another, yet many find themselves feeling like isolated islands in a sea of self-absorbed people. Take the time to discover that when you tune into others, your own personal trials will be minimized. Not only will you be distracted from your own circumstances, freeing God's hands to work without your intervention, but you will experience the joy of affecting someone else's life with the encouragement of an uplifting word. Try it. You might like it.

Practice Makes Perfect

*Those who plan what is good find
love and faithfulness.*

PROVERBS 14:22

What are your plans? Is a mate something that you simply want to acquire or do you really plan to be a gift in a man's life? Many who are of the mind-set that a man will complete their lives will be sorely disappointed. That is God's job. But to partner with someone and see him come alive, be a better man and a more productive person to the glory of God, now *that* is a wonderful mission statement for every woman to have. You can actually begin doing that now with the men who are already in your life. Practice makes perfect.

There is a joy in seeing the influence that you have in the life of anyone, but there is an extra bonus for sisters who sow in the lives of the brothers around them.

Plan to be a source of inspiration. To build up and not tear down. To exhort to good works. To sow future greatness. To assist them in being fruitful in every area of their lives. This is a good plan. God can now trust you with a life partner because you know what it is all about. In the meantime, there is the ever-present joy of seeing others blossom because of your presence in their lives. Again, it's about giving. And truly it is better to give than to receive. But the irony of it all is that if you give, you will receive! God sees to that.

Love requires risk.

Love requires feeling.

Love requires an honest response.

Love requires dying to yourself

listening,

learning,

serving,

and dying again.

A hundred times

or as many times as is required.

Are you ready for that?

It's Time

*There is a time for everything, and a season for every activity
under heaven: …a time to plant and a time to uproot…a time
to tear down and a time to build…a time to embrace and a
time to refrain…a time to search and a time to give up, a time to
keep and a time to throw away, a time to tear and a
time to mend…a time to love…*

ECCLESIASTES 3:1-3,5-8

Although we are anxious to understand, we know that
timing is everything. There is a time to prepare for the
love that God wants you to receive. Use it wisely.
There is a time to learn and experience the beauty of being
alone. It is in the alone time that we get to know ourselves. All
that we need, want, and don't want. Make a list. Discover your
own vulnerabilities and strengthen them. Face your fears and
defeat them. Embrace the Lover of your soul and refrain from
embracing unqualified strangers.

Plant new dreams and water them with prayer. Uproot un-
fruitful fantasies. Tear down every daydream and high, lofty
ideal that exalts itself against the knowledge of God and His
plan for your life and and then build on the destiny that He has
planted in your heart. Search for the truth and release every lie.
Give up all self-made designs and make room for God's will in
your life. Keep the good parts of your life and throw away the
clutter. The excess baggage that holds nothing beneficial. The
things that hinder you from moving forward and enjoying what

God has already made available to you. Tear off anything that is binding you to anger, depression, hopelessness, or resignation. Mend your heart and your spirit. Rehearse God's promises and allow the Holy Spirit to soothe your disappointments. Allow yourself to heal before you attempt to love. A broken heart shoots crooked arrows.

In other words, take the time that you've been given to become the best you that you can be. Redeem the time. Don't just tread water, go somewhere. Move forward and upward. Prepare yourself. Occupy your life fully until someone asks you to make room for them. Enjoy this season, for you know not when the weather will change. Yes, my sister, keep time and know that change is inevitable.

Time Will Tell

Daughters of Jerusalem, I charge you by the gazelles and by the
does of the field: Do not arouse or awaken love until it so desires.
SONG OF SONGS 2:7

The gazelle is known to be beautiful, small, graceful, and swift. But when we move in haste we can often find ourselves in trouble. One of the things I find interesting about the gazelle is its ability to focus on things close and far away at the same time. We, as females, also have these wonderful traits which must be balanced in order for us to gain joyful results from the decisions we make. Perhaps our Shulammite sister knew all of this when she shared this caution with her friends. Because we see things so quickly, we are tempted to move ahead of God. To stir up love, so to speak, if we even sense the possibility. But we must be willing to adapt to the feelings and desires of others. Love is flexible. Love is patient. Love that is really there isn't going anywhere; therefore, take your time. Test it. Observe it to discern its intentions. Is it lust or is it love? Only time will tell.

Think of it this way: You've been alone this long, why hurry now? Wait and get it right. Allow the heart to settle into a realistic space. Don't push, cajole, or try to make things happen before the appointed time. Remember there is a season for everything, including examination. Over and over Scripture encourages us to be very clear on where we are going and what we are doing. It is important to use your head, as well as your heart, in the issues of love. For something that is lasting, there should be no rush.

Love is not a feeling

it is a decision...

It is not love

that makes relationships last.

Rather, it is

our commitment

to the commitment we've made.

Therefore, give thought to making promises

lest you break them

and destroy the work of

your own hands...

Top Prize

I love those who love me,
and those who seek me find me.

PROVERBS 8:17

But whoever fails to find me harms himself;
all who hate me love death.

PROVERBS 8:36

Here you have two authorities talking on the subject of love. God and Wisdom. What they have to say holds true for us but it is something we must know in our very beings so that we don't grow sensitive to what we perceive as rejection.

God loves everyone. He calls and woos us to come and enjoy a relationship with Him. But only those who respond and look for Him find true love and experience the full benefit of what being in relationship with Him is all about. There is an intimacy that is enjoyed with those who respond to His loving embrace. What about the relationships in your life? Do you show a similar love? Yet we're also called to be discerning. Love everyone, yes, but only those who treasure and respond to your love should have the benefit of touching your heart in intimate places and have full access to your friendship, care, and affections.

Wisdom says whoever doesn't appreciate her, loses out. It's not *her* problem, it's *their* problem. They are not ready for the real thing! Every man you meet is not going to be ready for you. They will not appreciate what you have to offer; that is their problem and their loss. Feel sorry for them and all that they will be missing. This means that you must be convinced that you are the good thing that a man must find. He must seek you and do the work to claim you before he reaps the benefits.

If you are struggling with believing that you are a prize, a pearl of great price, then the work must begin there. Work it out, sister, until you believe it! Because the bottom line is you don't lose anything if someone doesn't recognize the gem that you are. The passersby are the ones who lose.

Revealing Light

*Jesus said to them, "If God were your Father, you would love me,
for I came from God and now am here."*

JOHN 8:42

*L*ight attracts light. Know that only those who love the
Light, or are seeking the Light, will be attracted to
you. Continue walking toward the Light, and they
will either join you or fade away. Even though Satan sends as-
signments into our lives—people who don't have our best in
mind—they cannot remain because darkness cannot remain in
the presence of light. Another wonderful reason to have no fear
and simply love. God will take care of your heart if you let Him.

I recall meeting a very interesting man a while back. He was
too good to be true. So I submitted him to God in prayer. My
specific prayer was this: "Lord, if this is the man You have chosen for me, I want You to talk to him about me like You spoke
to Joseph about Mary. However, if he is not for me and doesn't
have the right heart toward me, then I want You to remove him.
I want You to remove him so far that I won't be able to find him
if I look for him!" Well, shortly thereafter, the man vanished
into thin air! I was extremely upset until God reminded me that
I had asked Him to remove the guy if his thoughts toward me
were not honorable.

You see, we don't have to do the lifting and separating. The
Spirit of the Lord will do that. If you are truly living a committed life for the Lord, someone who is not living for the Lord

cannot remain in your presence. Unless it is his heart's desire to draw closer to God, he will not have more than a passing attraction for you. Don't get a complex. Let your life work for you. Know that what appears to be man's rejection is merely God's intervention and protection.

Beyond the Horizon

Because of the increase of wickedness,
the love of most will grow cold.

MATTHEW 24:12

The LORD will fulfill his purpose for me; your love, O LORD,
endures forever—do not abandon the works of your hands.

PSALM 138:8

It can be discouraging sometimes when we step back to take a mental scan of what is available on the man front. To tell the truth, the pickings look very slim. However, what your eyes see and what you have experienced in the past have absolutely nothing to do with God's plans and His ability to perform His promises. Perhaps we need to take our eyes off of the horizon line of our own rationalizations and get them fixed on the promises of He who knows where every good man is hidden.

Faith is being sure of what we hope for and certain of what we do not see, according to Hebrews 11:1. Your hope cannot be in men or in the surplus that we cannot see. It has to be in God's word to you. He is the only man who cannot lie. If He says it, He will do it. Go on, dare to hope again and know that He will finish every project He has started on your behalf. He will make sure that you have the love and companionship you need to live a joyful and productive life. And that, my friend, is that!

Love Notes from God

If I speak in the tongues of men and of angels, but have not love, I am only a resounding gong or a clanging cymbal. If I have the gift of prophecy and can fathom all mysteries and all knowledge, and if I have a faith that can move mountains, but have not love, I am nothing. If I give all I possess to the poor and surrender my body to the flames, but have not love, I gain nothing.

Love is patient, love is kind. It does not envy, it does not boast, it is not proud. It is not rude, it is not self-seeking, it is not easily angered, it keeps no record of wrongs. Love does not delight in evil but rejoices with the truth. It always protects, always trusts, always hopes, always perseveres. Love never fails.

But where there are prophecies, they will cease; where there are tongues, they will be stilled; where there is knowledge, it will pass away. For we know in part and we prophesy in part, but when perfection comes, the imperfect disappears.

When I was a child, I talked like a child, I thought like a child, I reasoned like a child. When I became a man, I put childish ways behind me. Now we see but a poor reflection as in a mirror; then we shall see face to face. Now I know in part; then I shall know fully, even as I am fully known. And now these three remain: faith, hope and love. But the greatest of these is love. Follow the way of love... (1 Corinthians 13–14:1)

The way of love is walking in complete maturity, not religiosity, from the heart.

Keep Hope Alive

And hope does not disappoint us, because God has poured out his love into our hearts by the Holy Spirit, whom he has given us.

ROMANS 5:5

Where we place our hope is crucial to our joy level. If hope deferred or unfulfilled makes our hearts sick, how do we allow this to happen in our lives? Perhaps we are hoping for the wrong thing. Perhaps we've told God specifically how our hope should be fulfilled. Perhaps in His foreknowledge, He knows that our perceived solution is not really the answer to the thing we crave.

Yet we continue to persist. Insisting that He do things our way. Give us that one specific man. And because God knows just any man is not a good and perfect gift, He withholds him, waiting for the appointed time to deliver the one who would truly make you happy. How much of our lives is spent growing frustrated and depressed over things that would make us more so?

If we put our hope in Him to give us what is best for us—a combination of what He knows we want mixed with what He knows we need—then our joy will be complete. This is where trust comes in and God's love becomes enough for us until He chooses to add to it through the arms of the one He has appointed to love us the way He does. Hmmm…sounds good to me. And definitely worth the wait.

Keep the Faith

The only thing that counts is faith
expressing itself through love.

GALATIANS 5:6

erhaps we have put the cart before the horse. We need to have faith first, love second. Why? To possess love without faith would leave us in torment, always checking to make sure that love is there. But the beautiful thing about love is you are able to rest in it. It permeates our lives in ways that cannot be denied when we have faith. Love is intangible in a sense: You must have faith in order to enjoy it. It is like the wind. You can't see it but you know it's there. Every once in a while it breezes gently across your face. At moments, it whips your hair and cools you. The wind blows in different degrees and intensities, yet no one doubts its existence. It is a common belief that the wind is real and manifests itself as it pleases. And we allow it to. But perhaps only because we have no control over it.

Love is like the wind. Every day is not a day filled with passion. Love ebbs and flows. Without faith, we would constantly press to substantiate love's existence in the hearts of those around us or a significant other. No, somewhere along the way we must choose faith over love. Believe that it is there in bottomless measures whether we feel it or not. And when the love of others is not apparent, God's love is faithfully present to fill

the void in us to overflowing so that we never lack. Faith pro-
claims love is...love is...love simply is. Faith removes the
pressure to find proof and that place of resting gives us immense
satisfaction and joy.

The Language of Love

This is how we know what love is: Jesus Christ laid down his life for us. And we ought to lay down our lives for our brothers...Let us not love with words or tongue but with actions and in truth.

1 JOHN 3:16,18

Many would say they feel loved based on what others do for them. One fondly remembers the day someone gave them flowers. Or soothed their pain. Or took the time to go out of their way to do something for them. They reflect upon these moments as expressions of true love. But can you really tell? Some people are nice for different reasons. To gain approval. To prove their own worth. To get something they want from you.

But the true language of love is willing sacrifice. This is seldom thought of as we pursue finding the one true love of our lives. How much are you willing to sacrifice to have what you want? Your life as you know it to accommodate the interest of another? A dream that would interfere with your beloved's? This is important. This is big. Many a new mother struggles with her own sense of identity during the time that her career is put aside for the sake of that newborn. Think about what you would be willing to sacrifice for the love you want. Now translate that into acts of kindness in the lives of those who are available to be loved in your world at this very moment.

Love speaks through actions, not words. Every sacrifice, every act of giving is a resounding message from the heart of the giver that needs no explanation. Who can argue with sacrifice? Who can argue with kindness and consideration? Who can doubt the love of one who gives unconditionally? Words are one thing, but actions are superior, for they reveal the heart of God to those around us. If we truly love and do nothing to show it, then we lie to ourselves as well as to others.

After you've learned the language of love, you will have no trouble translating it into real-life love experiences right where you live, right now.

Love in Action

Live a life of love, just as Christ loved us and gave himself up for us as a fragrant offering and sacrifice to God.

EPHESIANS 5:2

Every single day we get countless opportunities to live a life of love. To reach out to someone. To lift a spirit. To encourage a soul. To simply compliment someone who might not even be aware of her own beauty that day. The ability to make others smile is amazing. It is like giving flowers to strangers who would be overwhelmed by such a pleasant surprise.

Christ came with the determination to liberate the captive, heal the sick and wounded, and ransom all of mankind. Giving of Himself was His love language. What is your love language? Is it treating someone to lunch? Drying someone's tears? Making someone feel better? If we are imitators of Christ, our love language should also be giving to the point of sacrifice. At times, giving of yourself will not be convenient. Take the time to listen anyway. Give anyway. Reach out anyway. Love anyway. The sense of accomplishment after the deed is done cannot be measured. The returns are intangible but felt in bountiful measures. The joy of knowing your life matters. Your gift of love matters...and most of all *you* matter because you've made yourself available as a vessel to continue the conversation that God wants to have with those around you...and for that you are truly loved.

Going the Distance

*May the Lord direct your hearts into God's love
and Christ's perseverance.*

2 THESSALONIANS 3:5

Love and perseverance go hand in hand because all love must be tested. Ooh, we hate that word! It speaks of trial and pain and all the things that we don't like. Yet this is why love must be firmly entrenched in God first. When our hearts are firmly entrenched in His loving hands, kept safe and secure from all that can buffet them, then we will be able to weather the storms that try our love. Allow God, and the knowledge of His love for you, to strengthen your resolve to love with abandon.

Remember, the enemy of our souls wants to rob you of the love that you should experience. He wants to destroy your heart and kill your expectations of ever having a divine love life. Don't let him. Stand firm in your determination to love. No matter how difficult the way may be. No matter how fearsome the journey. Know that you will never come out of a love experience empty handed. There is always a priceless lesson or a life-changing experience birthed in the exchange. Try to have the determination that Christ had to reach and embrace us.

Love goes the distance to the point of death if necessary. Love toughs it out and makes it through the difficult places. Love does not give up! Jesus did not give up on us; we can't give up on those around us. This does not mean becoming a victim of abuse. Exercise love through prayer, example, encouragement, and inspiration. Remember, anything worth having is worth fighting for. Don't grow weary of the struggle. Refresh yourself with the love that God lavishly makes available to you and then get back in the game.

Live Abundantly

Mercy, peace and love be yours in abundance.

JUDE 2

If it is your Father's good pleasure to give you the kingdom, then truly He wants you to experience the best of everything in abundance. He is generous with what we long for most—mercy, peace, and love. What man does not furnish, He is able to supply to the point of overflowing. There is never a shortage of these longed-after gifts when we rest in His arms.

Feeling a little empty? Ask the Author of love and pleasure to give you a refill. He is able and willing to answer the cry of your heart and satisfy your deepest longings.

Why is He so willing to keep these treasured blessings on reserve for us? Because it was always His intention for us to have them. And remember, whenever you pray in the Father's perfect will, that is a prayer He will answer. So ask, and ask often, for mercy, peace, and love—not just in small portions, but in abundance.

Just Wait

Keep yourselves in God's love as you wait for the mercy
of our Lord Jesus Christ to bring you to eternal life.

JUDE 21

This is great advice across the board. Keep yourself in God's love as you wait for anything! A true love relationship. A promotion in your job. The opportunity you've always wanted. The list goes on and on. If you are kept in His love, you won't grow weary or anxious. The assurance of His ever-present love will keep you in remembrance of the fact that He knows what's best for you and He's working on it. If you've asked Him for bread, surely He won't give you a stone. Sometimes in our haste to put out the gnawing fire of longing within ourselves, we select stones hoping that they are bread. Yet God, in His omniscience is able to call a stone a stone. So passionate is He about giving you the best, He will discard the stones rather than serve them to you.

No, my friend, He, like the owner of a renowned vineyard, will serve nothing before it is time. Wait on Him. Know that He loves you. He wants what is best for you and will not settle for anything less than that even if you will. Just wait...

A friend chastised me once by telling me that waiting on God is not climbing into His lap then peering over His shoulder every five minutes to see if the thing I desire is coming. I didn't want to hear it at the time, but it is true. Waiting on God is not just enjoying being in the center of His love, it is also serving Him joyfully to the point of distraction. Yes, you can actually be distracted from your own longings if you focus on pleasing Him! His pleasure becomes your desire and it transcends all the other things you have been hoping and praying for. As your heart joins with His, certain desires will change, but those that are in accordance with God's desires will be fulfilled. The bottom line? Joy. Here, now, and forevermore.

Truth in Love

*Above all, love each other deeply,
because love covers over a multitude of sins.*

1 PETER 4:8

Do everything in love.

1 CORINTHIANS 16:14

If we are motivated by what we want from people, our love flow will go up and down to the point of being maddening. We will be besieged by the shortcomings of others and their disappointing behavior toward us. But if our focus becomes simply loving, grace will come to deal with the weaknesses of others. And they will respond to that grace with changes we find miraculous.

When we love unconditionally, we release people to be who they are. In loving, we finally see that no one was made to be all that we expect them to be, and we accept that fact graciously. Love is not blind, contrary to what the world propagates. It is realistic and forgiving. It does not excuse sin. It simply refocuses what threatens to become judgment in search of a solution. A soft answer turns away wrath, while an offended brother or sister is harder to win than a fortified city.... If we come from a place of love, even in correction, a spoonful of sugar will help the medicine go down.

Have you been offended? Speak the truth in love. Been disappointed and let down by someone's attitude or behavior?

Speak the truth in love. Feel as if you are giving more than you are getting? Speak the truth in love and be open to the other person's response. It will give you cues on how to measure your offerings. Love, but give others the time and space to love you back. Do not demand, do not push, be honest in your sentiments, and don't berate others for what they are not capable of or willing to do at the time. Release them to love. See the truth and accept it lovingly. Strengthen rather than tear down through harsh criticism. Cover them with encouragement rather than expose their weaknesses. That is the Holy Spirit's job, and He does it very well. This is an exercise of self-discipline that can prove difficult and sometimes leave you feeling powerless. But the results are sweet and lasting. Your healthy heart will thank you for it. You might ask in exasperation as you ponder the situation in your life, "Well, what's a girl to do?" My answer is, "Take a step back and love, girl. Simply love and let everything else fall into, or out of, place."

Remember above all things

    that Jesus is the Lover of your soul

which is where all love begins and ends...

Men...

sat·is·fac·tion \ˌsat-əs-'fak-shən\ *n* [ME, tr. MF, tr. LL *satisfac-tion-, satisfactio,* fr. L., reparation, amends, fr. *satisfactus,* pp. of *satis-facere* to satisfy] (14c) **1 a :** the payment through penance of the temporal punishment incurred by a sin **b :** reparation for sin that meets the demands of divine justice **2 a :** fulfillment of a need or want **b :** the quality or state of being satisfied : CONTENTMENT **c :** a source or means of enjoyment : GRATIFICATION **3 a :** compensation for a loss or injury : ATONEMENT, RESTITUTION **b :** the discharge of a legal obligation or claim **c :** VINDICATION **4 :** convinced assurance or certainty ⟨proved to the ∼ of the court⟩

Sat-is-fy \'sat-təs-fī/ –fied; -fying vb **1a:** to carry out the terms of (as a contract) **b:** to meet a financial obligation to **2:** to make reparation to (an injured party) **3:** to make happy: PLEASE **b:** to gratify to the full: APPEASE **4 a:** CONVINCE **b:** to put an end to (doubt or uncertainty) : DISPEL **5:** to conform to (as specifications): be adequate to (an end in view) **Syn 1** SATISFY, FULFILL, MEET, ANSWER: to measure up to a set of criteria or requirements.

sa·to·ri \sə-'tōr-ē, sä-, -'tór-\ *n* [Jp] (1727) : a state of intuitive illumina-tion sought in Zen Buddhism

sa·trap \'sā-ˌtrap *also* 'sa-ˌtrap *or* 'sa-trəp\ *n* [ME, fr. L *satrapes,* fr. Gk *satrapēs,* fr. OPer *xshathrapāvan,* lit., protector of the dominion] (14c) **1 :** the governor of a province in ancient Persia **2 a :** RULER **b :** a subordinate official : HENCHMAN

Getting Real

All right, ladies, it's time to get real. Down to the nitty-gritty. Where the rubber hits the road. You got it. We're getting ready to talk man talk. Mmhm…can't live with them, can't live without them, can't kill them. They're real. They're difficult. They're mysterious. But really not that hard to figure out. Hard to change, yes. Perhaps because that's not our job! How far are you willing to go to have the relationship you want with one of these elusive creatures? We'll find out.

It's time to get a realistic perspective on men, love, and our own hearts. We've been up, down, and turned around enough. At the end of the day, most of the fault is ours. Now it is time to get in the winner's seat and stay there as we take a look at our desires, fantasies, and how it really is. So if you're willing, we can get honest and real together. Hopefully you'll come out of this with a lot of joy heaped on top of a mound of revelation that is sure to set you free.

Holy Wholeness

"Sir," the invalid replied, "I have no one to help me into the pool when the water is stirred. While I am trying to get in, someone else goes down ahead of me."

JOHN 5:7

*T*he story goes there was a man who had been paralyzed by his infirmity for 38 years. Jesus approached him and asked him if he wanted to be whole. Instead of the obvious answer, yes, the man blamed his condition on the lack of someone to assist him in reaching a state of wholeness. He completely missed the fact that the secret of his wholeness and restoration was standing before him. He was focused on man. He was focused on the pool. He was focused on everything but Jesus and almost missed his deliverance and transformation...

Hmmm.... What are you focused on? What is robbing you of your wholeness and joy? Are you paralyzed by the longing for a man to make you whole? Have you overlooked the love and wholeness that is already available to you? Jesus is standing before you asking the same question, "Do you want to be whole?" What will your answer be?

Wholeness is not found in a man or the abundance of things that we possess. It is not even found in the pool of love that we thought would wash away all of our bad experiences and past hurts. A love relationship simply brings new tests and trials to be overcome with the help of our Savior. No, my sister, wholeness can only be found in our relationship with our heavenly fiancé, Jesus Christ.

Yes! He is your fiancé! He is off building you a house and promises to return for you. In the meantime, He has sent the Best Man, the Holy Spirit, to make sure you have everything you need until His return. He will not leave you comfortless or broken. Perhaps you've been looking for love in all the wrong places. I can relate. Turn your eyes upon Jesus, the Lover of your soul, and begin to cultivate an intimate relationship with Him. When He fills you with His spiritual love, earthly love will come—from more places than you expect.

Living Water

The fact is, you have had five husbands,
and the man you now have is not your husband.
What you have just said is quite true.

JOHN 4:18

She was disillusioned, this Samaritan woman at the well. She had given many men her mind, her body, and perhaps even her heart. By the time she met Jesus, she had heard it all—every smooth rap—and His offer of water that would finally satisfy her was just another line. First of all, no one else had been qualified to soothe the wounds that lay deep within her. They had nothing to draw from but their own emptiness and pain. How could what He had to offer be any different or better than what everyone else had offered? Love, security, a nice house, a happy future, *blah, blah, blah,* forever and ever amen…

She didn't want to hear it. She had been there, done that. She felt unworthy of the love she longed for. She had been used and abused. She was tired. She would settle for what physical solace she could find and forget about ever being deeply satisfied. However, Jesus was determined to capture her heart, so He gently persisted. Something about His manner caught her attention, giving her one last glimmer of hope. She would try His water. After all, she had tried everything else. Could she be any more disappointed than she already was?

She had nothing. A man yes, but really nothing. And the man she was with was not her husband. Jesus didn't condemn her. He lovingly acknowledged the truth of her statement. Six men and she was still thirsty, still not satisfied. Well!

Some of us have had one man too many. Our hearts have been shattered, our spirits weakened by our own thirst that refuses to be satisfied. We've grown disillusioned and apathetic, failing to believe that love is possible for us at this stage in the game. We have too much baggage, too much pain to even respond to someone who might actually come offering the real thing.

To you Jesus says, "Come and drink." Drink from the love that has always been there for you. Waters that run deep and unending. Doesn't that sound good? Most of us have experienced looking for love in all the wrong places. Let me point you to the right place—the heart of Jesus.

You cannot discern what real love is until you have experienced it. Then you'll know it's the real thing. Those who are trained to identify counterfeit money are never shown fake bills. They are told to study the real thing. Every line and indentation. They scrutinize it so thoroughly that the moment anything not genuine is thrust before them, they don't miss a beat. They recognize it immediately. In order to *get* true love you must *know* true love. You must know what it feels like, what it looks like, what it sounds like. Only then will you be able to avoid and disqualify mere imitations. Imitations that leave you more thirsty and needy than before.

Settle for nothing less than what you experience with Christ—faithfulness, peace, joy beyond measure, and blessings that add no sorrow.

Balanced Perspective

He (Jesus) took the blind man by the hand and led him outside the village. When he had spat on the man's eyes and put his hands on him, Jesus asked, "Do you see anything?" He looked up and said, "I see people; they look like trees walking around." Once more Jesus put his hands on the man's eyes. Then his eyes were opened, his sight was restored, and he saw everything clearly. Jesus sent him home, saying, "Don't go (back) into the village."

MARK 8:23-26

Sometimes we have been in a state of mind so long that we can't see anything different. If the area of men or finding a mate has loomed large, and has become an overwhelming mountain you can't see your way over, it's time to get another touch from God. Keep revisiting the issue with Him as much as you need to. Sometimes once is not enough. Be determined to get to the point where you come into balance and see everything from the right perspective.

Could it be that the issue of men has grown out of proportion in your thoughts? Is it stopping you from seeing the big picture for your life? Are you putting life on hold and failing to enjoy all that you can right now because you are waiting for the perfect mate to complete your life? It is time to step outside of yourself and get free.

Men are wonderful, and at the right time they can be a beautiful addition to the life that you and God have created together. But until then there is a lot to be joyful about. Good health, wonderful friends, and family. Countless opportunities to experience something new and interesting every day. But if men are like trees in your life, you won't be able to enjoy the view.

Explore a new way of looking at the life you presently live. Move forward and don't look back.

Before you get excited about the cover,

you had better read the contents.

Filling the Void

Your desire will be for your husband,
and he will rule over you.

GENESIS 3:16

When Eve voted to act independently from God, suddenly she was aware of the void that He had filled. It was a space so cavernous even Adam couldn't fill it. She did not die for partaking of the forbidden fruit, but a feeling worse than death followed that first bite. She experienced an inward death—death of a true love connection that could only be maintained by the Spirit of God. She suffered the death of a connection she did not fully understand. She discovered that all those wonderful feelings of oneness were completed by God Himself, not Adam. When God pronounced the consequences for her disobedience, the damage became apparent.

Now Eve would long for Adam to fill the space that God had once filled. Of course, he would never be able to do this. He wasn't created to take God's place in her heart. Her desire for completion and fulfillment from her man would become overwhelming to the point of ruling over her. *Her desire for her husband would rule over her.* There it is. Still being perpetuated today. It is important for you to know that because of the death of Jesus Christ this fate no longer belongs to you. Your desire for intimacy with Christ cancels out the void. It puts you back in the driver's seat of your desires. Desires should not dominate you. They should not affect your joy level.

How much time, energy, and emotional stress do you put into worrying about having a mate? How much of your conversation is about a man or the lack thereof? Are your friends strangely silent, or do they sound like a broken record when you bring up the subject? It is time to take those desires and lay them at the foot of the cross, where they can no longer reign over you. Allow the Lord to fill the void within you. Accept the liberty you now have to be an independent woman in Him.

Remember, "the two shall become one." In God's equation, two halves do not make a whole. Two whole people are able to become one. Two halves result in one big mess of a relationship that may or may not stand the test of time and trial. Allow God to be the answer to the missing piece in your life. Get full. Get happy. Get whole. And then get ready to receive the one who can only add to the joy that is already resident within you.

Never Alone

The LORD God said, "It is not good for the man to be alone.
I will make a helper suitable for him."

GENESIS 2:18

*I*nteresting! Adam never broached the subject of needing a mate with God. God decided when it was time. Have you allowed God to work His schedule in your life or have you put Him on deadline? Notice that God did not say, "It is not good for the man to be lonely." Adam was alone, in the sense of not having a human companion, but he was not lonely. There is a difference. Adam dwelt in the presence of God and felt no lack. As we dwell in the presence of God, He divinely decides what we are lacking. We should be so caught up in the sufficiency of His goodness that what we lack isn't even apparent to us. Allow me to give you the true definition of lonely—the absence of God. You cannot miss what you've never had. Therefore Adam did not miss having someone else in his life. He already had someone—God.

There is a peace that few know. The joy of reveling in God's company. Once you experience it you won't allow anyone or anything to mess it up. It will keep you from accepting just anything or anyone in your life. Why? Because though you are alone, you are not lonely.

Adam had been given an assignment. Be fruitful, multiply, have dominion over every living thing, and subdue all things in the earth. In other words, add to God's creation, supervise it, and keep it all in order. Adam did a good job with the latter, but he needed help with the first part of the assignment. He could not be fruitful and multiply on his own. It would take a special person to walk in sync with Adam and help him complete his God-ordained mission. This person had to be fashioned especially for him.

What you need to understand is that the man God has for you has been given an assignment. God has spent your whole life fashioning you into a helper that will be suitable for your mate. He is already out there. God is finishing a work in him as well before joining you together. Allow God to train him, groom him, and prepare him for you. That does not mean that he will be perfect when he arrives. Whole, yes; perfect, no. On an assignment, yes; able to complete it alone, no. Are you getting this? Marriage and having a mate are not just about you. It is about a partnership for God's glory. To the furtherance of completing His plan. In the meantime, learn to discern the difference between being alone and being lonely.

Perfect Match

*So the man gave names to all the livestock,
the birds of the air and all the beasts of the field.
But for Adam no suitable helper was found.*

GENESIS 2:20

When we give names to the people and circumstances in our lives we come up with some pretty interesting things. Let's see, we call Mr. Wrong "Mr. Right." Things that are unacceptable we say are "workable"... shall I go on? What was the point of this whole naming exercise? It gave man practice in exercising his authority. After all, God didn't change the names of anything after Adam named them.

Let me tell you something, my dear sister. If you want to name Mr. Wrong "Mr. Right," God will not interrupt you. He has given you free will and authority to exercise it as you may. Until you are ready to hear what God has to say about that man in your life He will let you name him, claim him, and frame him anyway you please. Don't mistake God's silence for approval.

Yes, Adam named the animals, but it was obvious they were all coupled up as like kind. There was none that bore a resemblance to him. None of the animals could help him complete the assignment that God had given him.

So your mate hasn't shown up yet? Perhaps he is still naming the animals. We've named a few ourselves—various dogs, frogs, and beasts, but when the exercise is over the verdict is the same—there is none suitable. Accept that and wait until there is. Don't try to dress up an animal and make it into something it isn't. Call a spade a spade. "This person cannot help me be all that God has created me to be." Name them what they are— "not for you"—and move on in the expectancy that God has created one of like kind for you.

Let It Rest

So the Lord God caused the man to fall into a deep sleep; and while he was sleeping, he took one of the man's ribs and closed up the place with flesh. Then the Lord God made a woman from the rib he had taken out of the man, and he brought her to the man. The man said, "This is now bone of my bones and flesh of my flesh; she shall be called 'woman', for she was taken out of man."

GENESIS 2:21-23

So...after Adam had named all the animals, he may have noticed all had mates but himself. It was then that God caused him to enter into a state of rest. Perhaps this is the secret for us. If you have found it difficult to be at rest about this mate thing, ask God to help you enter into His rest. Adam slept and God went to work. This could be a part of the secret. Let go and let God! He seems to do a better job when we are out of the way.

Believe you me, when God goes about securing your mate, that man will be perfect for you. He will be fashioned to complete not *you*, (that should already have happened in Christ) but the puzzle of your life. The missing pieces of your character and personality. He will take you to another level of relationship with Christ because, through this man, you will learn the secret of true oneness. He will be your mirror. Do you know why he will be able to reflect and reveal who you are? *Because he will know you.* God will put a knowing of who you are—your needs and desires—deep within his spirit, and he will recognize that you are his missing rib! The one he has been looking for.

You will not need to inform him that you're the one for him because he will *know* that instinctively. Eve did not go up to Adam and tell him, "Wake up, Adam. The Lord said you are my husband!" She merely stood in the frame of God's timing and allowed herself to be recognized. She stood secure in the fact that she was a complete and desirable work crafted by the Master's hand. Fearfully and wonderfully made. Why wouldn't he want her? She was perfect for him. Assigned to help him. To be a physical extension of God's love for him. And God didn't wake Adam up a minute before He was completely finished with Eve.

How do you think he recognized her? Firstly, God presented her to him. Which means God revealed her to him. There was no denying it. No need for fasting, praying, and getting friends in spiritual agreement to convince him on her part. She came complete with everything that Adam realized he wanted and needed. Eve experienced the joy of being recognized and chosen by Adam.

Are you allowing God to finish you? Or are you rearranging His design? Are you submitting to the paces of training to be a suitable mate for your husband? Are you clear on your purpose as a woman, as a creation of the Most High God? Before you look for the man, be made perfect in God's love, know your assignment, and be equipped for the mission.

Back to the Garden

The man and his wife were both naked,
and they felt no shame.

GENESIS 2:25

ow refreshing it must have been. Two people, Adam and Eve, standing before one another with no past experiences, nothing to feel self-conscious about. All they could do was celebrate God and each other. No past mistakes stood between them. No doubts about their own desirability, worthiness for true love, lies entrenched in their psyche, bad examples of other failed relationships, nothing to weigh their love down. They were free to simply love! No one has been in such a state of utopia since. However, God is willing to wash, heal, and restore what has been broken and bruised in our hearts and give us new beginnings. He is able to heal memories and speak words of truth about who we are in Him. We can return back to the Garden—whole, cleansed, unashamed, and no longer encumbered by our past.

Can we talk about excess baggage, pain, shame, and other things? Get rid of them. Take the time you have alone to sort through the baggage and get rid of things you cannot use to nurture the next potentially healthy relationship. Don't ruin a good man because of the last bad man in your life.

God wants us to be transparent with the man He presents us to. Vulnerable, trusting, and open to love. But we can only get there if we allow the Spirit of God to lead us beside His cool waters where we can rest and our faith can be restored. We can return to the Garden carrying no burdens, only a heart that is open to love.

A Good Thing

*He who finds a wife finds what is good and
receives favour from the LORD.*

PROVERBS 18:22

Are you a good thing? Are you a well-rounded woman? Can you balance business with pleasure? Have you mastered the art of encouragement? Making a house a home? Cooking a meal that will find its way to his heart? Are you filled with wisdom and joy? Are your affairs set in order? Are your finances under control? Do you have something to bring to the party? Are you able to let a man be a man? Do you enjoy being a woman?

What is one way a man can obtain the favor of the Lord? Through having the right woman by his side. It is through her encouragement, inspiration, and quiet strength that a man can become more of what God created him to be. She creates an oasis for his mind. A place of refreshing for his spirit. A safe place for his heart to rest. A pleasant garden for his body. With all of this accomplished, a man is prepared to face the world. His head is together. When his head is together, his business is together. He becomes known as a man of sound character, integrity, and excellence, and he wins favor among his peers. What do you get out of the deal? You get to enjoy the prosperity and the blessings that his good virtues bring. Good and fair payment for your labor.

A good woman taps into her man, senses his moods, and knows how to soothe the savage beast. She covers her man in prayer, interceding for him daily. Lifting, exhorting, and gently prodding him onward toward the finish line. She knows how to appeal to all of his senses. She is soft to the touch. She appeals to his taste with fine dishes. She smells nice. She looks good. Her voice should be music to his ears.

Are you cultivating these traits? Not just for him, but for yourself? There is something irresistible about a woman who is all woman. She enjoys the experience of being who she is and others are drawn to her without knowing why. They will simply say, "I don't know...there's just something about her." In turn, the man in your life will love you for it. Because of his obedience to God, he falls right in line with God's command about how he should treat you. For his willing obedience, God answers his prayers. Truly, it is the little things that bring big returns.

So be a good thing. Enjoy the process of learning how to cultivate traits that will make you the catalyst for your man being covered in favor!

An empowered woman + An empowered man = God's glory being fully manifested in the earth

Be Open

He looked up to heaven and with a deep sigh said to him,
"Ephphatha!" (which means, "Be opened!").

MARK 7:34

What type of man are you looking for? That is the question. How open have you been to different options? One thing I know about God is He never does the expected. Therefore, be open. Every woman that I know who is happily married has said the same thing. "Girl, he was not what I was looking for. I would have never believed I would be this happy with him."

One national newsstand magazine did a feature on older women and how happy they were with younger men. More and more people are crossing racial lines. Age lines, race lines, denominational lines. The verdict is out that the choices are limited. We must not lower our standards, but we should broaden our options.

Consider what you *need* versus what you think you *want*. You may *want* the rich man but you really *need* the man who loves you. He may not be the high-powered business mogul, just a simple, secure man who loves the ground you walk upon. If you are the woman God created you to be, you can be instrumental in causing this man to prosper.

This brings to mind the story of a successful executive woman who married her gardener. She met this kind, sensitive man who loved her deeply and married him, much to the dismay of her friends and social circle. She didn't care. Her rationale was she wanted someone at home when she got there. She was happy. After they were married, she began to encourage her husband to expand his gardening practice because he had such a great eye. This gardener developed into the owner of a major landscaping business—a very successful man.

The moral of the story? God rarely gives us a finished product. He gives us diamonds in the rough whose sparkle may not yet be apparent. Then He supplies us with the ingredients and the tools to craft them into something beautiful. Always be open to the incredible possibilities.

Take this simple test:

What you want:

- ❏ Someone godly

- ❏ Someone handsome and charismatic

- ❏ Someone successful

- ❏ Someone intelligent

- ❏ Someone with a good sense of humor

- ❏ Someone romantic

- ❏ Someone interesting

What you need:

- ❏ Someone who loves, hears, and *obeys* God

- ❏ Someone honest and sensitive

- ❏ Someone responsible

- ❏ Someone consistent

- ❏ Someone hardworking

- ❏ Someone who wants to be a husband and a family man

- ❏ Someone who loves and cherishes you above everything but God

Things to consider:

- Generally speaking, with a few exceptions, the high-powered successful man will be too busy being successful to give you the love and attention you are sure to crave. Are you willing to sacrifice the time that he won't be able to devote to you?

- The man who is a mover and shaker is not looking for another mover and shaker. He is looking for someone to be there when he finally has down time. Are you that woman or do you have dreams of your own that you would like to have a spouse celebrate, if not support?

- Successful men are usually achievers for two reasons:

    1. Either they are driven by insecurities, fear of failure, or their aspirations are a form of compensation for unresolved issues.

    2. They are sold out to God's vision for their lives and have prospered under His direction or the encouragement of those that God has placed in their lives.

After discerning which category he is in, you must be realistic about how much energy will be directed toward his vision and away from you. Are you willing to share a man with his vision?

So, do you want a life partner and companion, or a husband and a benefactor? Just asking!

Gems in Disguise

"Nazareth! Can anything good come from there?" Nathanael asked.

JOHN 1:46

Remember that Jesus, because He became a man in the incarnation, looked like other men. He rather blended into the crowd. In fact, He was broke as far as anyone knew. No fabulous wardrobe. He said He didn't have anyplace to lay His head. No house?! He had to go fishing to pay his taxes. He didn't have a regular day job. Yet He was the King of Kings and the Lord of Lords in the form of a common man. Is this someone who you would have been interested in?

If that isn't an object lesson, I don't know what is. Many a woman was drawn to him. Why? He was caring, sensitive, wise, strong yet gentle, perceptive to their deepest and most secret desires. He touched them in a way no other man had. He was understanding, not condemning, of their past mistakes, and they knew He loved them. He was willing to die for them.

Now that is a man I could love! Why don't we meet more men like that? Perhaps because they don't come in the package we want or expect. We overlook them every day. Decent, hard-working, quiet, unglamourous men…hmm, gems in disguise that could use the polish of a woman's touch. Have you ever noticed that most married men are more attractive than single ones? Their wives all say the same thing, "Chil', he wasn't like that when I got him!" Stop looking for the ready-made package.

There aren't any no matter how old they are! I urge you to kill the fantasy and examine the heart of a man before discarding unobvious treasure. I believe more women would be happily married if they followed this advice.

Are we passing models of Jesus by on a daily basis because they don't look or dress the way we want them to? Not interesting enough? How do you know? Have you really taken the time to dig beneath the surface? Still waters run deep. The Bible tells us that when we see our husband, Jesus, again that He will be wondrous to behold. I believe it will be the look of love in His eyes that will make Him so beautiful to us. We have been made beautiful because of His sacrifice for us, and we will be made flawless by His presence and glory. Through the eyes of love, an ordinary man becomes beautiful and we become more beautiful as they cover us with their love. Have you ever seen the glow on someone's face who is deeply in love? 'Nuf said. Until we are united with our mates, we are in pre-construction—works in progress. Dare to cast away your past wish list, get real, and dig deeper. You might be surprised at what you find.

My mentor and friend P. Bunny Wilson (author of *Knight in Shining Armor*) tells me all the time that she believes most women already know their mate. Hmmm…are you overlooking a friend you adore because he is not your type? May I ask exactly what is your type? Has your type ever been the type who will commit to you?

I am reminded of the joke about the man who was perishing in a flood. "Oh, Lord, save me!" he cried out. A plane came by and offered him a ride, to which he replied, "No thanks, I'm waiting for the Lord to save me." A boat came by and pleaded with him to hop in. "Oh no, the Lord will save me," he exclaimed. Well, he died and went to heaven and with great consternation he asked the Lord, "Lord, why didn't you save me?" To which the Lord replied, "I sent the plane, I sent the boat, and you wouldn't get in!"

Could it be that we are praying for a mate and when He sends a candidate our way we kick him to the side and say, "No, Lord, not that one!" Again, just asking…

You ask for a cup of water. I give it to you in a cup that you would not have selected. Will you not drink? Don't confuse the water with the cup. The water is what you need and desire. The cup can be cleaned up, painted, or changed.

Crazy Thing About Love

*There are three things that are too amazing for me, four that
I do not understand: the way of an eagle in the sky, the way of a
snake on a rock, the way of a ship on the high seas,
and the way of a man with a maiden.*

PROVERBS 30:18-19

It is remarkable how an eagle stays aloft in the sky because he does not flap his wings, he merely rides the current of the winds. How does a snake stay on top of a rock? It's slippery, the rock is slippery. How does a ship stay on top of the water? We often wonder how such a heavy object can float upon a surface that is not solid. I'm sure if planes had been invented back then, Solomon would have mentioned how amazing it is that they can fly. Likewise, men and women are sometimes hard to figure out and often defy logic! No man is the same. No woman is the same. In the face of sometimes dubious, often outrageous and nonsensical circumstances, love flourishes in spite of all that wars against it working out.

Though you must use your head in love, you must not over-intellectualize it. Love defies logic, even as the existence of God and some of His ways often defy common sense and challenge our understanding. In spite of our sin He loves us and wants us to be His own. He loves the unlovely. He sees worth in the broken. He celebrates the discarded. He promotes the unqualified. He looks beyond our faults and sees our needs.... His ways are past finding out!

The way of love is the way of God. Love covers a multitude of shortcomings and sins. Love covers what selfishness and greed expose. Love, who can understand it? It looks past us and all of our fears, questions, and "isms" and just loves anyway. It can be painful, hilarious, soothing, terrible, binding, or without reserve. It is a complex thing. The world would reduce it to simply a burst of emotion that can change from moment to moment or even cease to be. But for the believer, it must be more than that. God's love never fails or quits. It is a commitment to stand firm and endure, support, nurture, and cover the object of our affections no matter what. Even when the feelings have died, the commitment to love remains.

How do we do that? Trust in the Lord with all our hearts and lean not on our own understanding, the proverb goes. When you can't figure out that man, turn him over to the Lord and allow Him to reveal the heart of the matter to you. As children of light, there is never any need to walk in the darkness of confusion, frustration, and worry. When we reach the end of our understanding, God's knowledge and wisdom are there to meet us. To expose the hidden things and give us workable solutions. To carry us through the difficult places of our relationships and restore the joy of loving.

Love...who can figure it out? God can.

Soul Food

With persuasive words she led him astray; she seduced him with
her smooth talk. All at once he followed her like an ox going to
the slaughter, like a deer stepping into a noose till an arrow
pierces his liver, like a bird darting into a snare,
little knowing it will cost him his life.

PROVERBS 7:21-23

*L*adies, we have got to be careful how we use our power with the men in our lives. If this woman was able to seduce this man to do the wrong thing, consider seducing a man to do the right thing. Don't lead the man to death, lead him to life. God will hold you responsible. Little did this woman in Proverbs know that she was merely preparing the path for her own death as well.

There is no doubt this was a lonely woman, probably married to one of those businessmen we talked about. Maybe her husband was away on a business trip. In spite of all that he had given her, like a fabulous house with wonderful trappings, she went out looking for love in all the wrong places and found someone who suited her fancy. She came on to him and took him home and, well…you know the rest. In my imagination, I see them the next morning. Him leaving with no real promises of returning. Remember the song, "Will You Still Love Me Tomorrow?" That about sums it up. Oh, the agony of living in uncertainty over love! Initiating it, always putting in more than she gets out. Finding fleeting glimpses of pleasure, then being left to feel used, robbed, discarded. It is too heavy a burden to bear. She returns to her empty home, which now feels emptier than before. Still not feeling the love she desires. When you sow to the flesh all you get is temporary gratification. And the spirit within you cries, "Is that all there is? There must be more..."

This is the consequence of not following God's road map to love. As women of God, we must lead the men in our lives to higher heights in God where they will find life and true love to share with us. If your desperation for a mate leads you to put more focus on yourself than on the things of God, you will end up with a mess on your hands that will eventually pan out to nothing. Remember God first, all other things second. A man who is committed to God will be committed to you. A man who won't break God's heart won't break your heart. It will be up to you to establish the course of your relationship with a man once he has expressed interest. As the verse says: The man followed the woman's invitation.

Yes, it is true that probably the first thing that caught his eye was your external qualities. Men are driven by sight. But the physical attraction soon wears off. What will *keep* him is the internal stuff. The light from within. Allow him to fall in love with the God in you before distracting him with all the other things you feel you need to offer him to hold his attention. In our limited human state, we only have so much to offer, but God's supply of interesting and new delights is endless. He allows us to tap into them in order to keep love fresh and exciting.

Be realistic about the fact that there will always be someone prettier and wittier—have something that is unique to you. Develop your capacity to encourage him and make him feel good about himself when he is with you. Men fall in love with you based on how they feel when they are with you. Therefore, make investments in him that are lasting, where you're sure to reap a joyful return. Feed his spirit. Feed his mind. Cause him to crave your presence by constantly feeding him life.

Purity Under Pressure

You are a garden locked up, my sister, my bride; you are a spring enclosed, a sealed fountain. Your plants are an orchard of pomegranates with choice fruits, with henna and nard, nard and saffron, calamus and cinnamon, with every kind of incense tree, with myrrh and aloes and all the finest spices. You are a garden fountain, a well of flowing water streaming down from Lebanon.

SONG OF SONGS 4:12-15

Quiet as it is kept, men rejoice when they find a woman who is living in purity. Keeping herself just for him. Perhaps it is an ego thing for them to have what no one else has been able to get. This is a rare find. This one thing causes a woman's value to shoot up faster than the stock market on an exemplary day. Many are no longer virgins. There's no need to fret. Know and believe that you have been restored back to this state by the blood of the Lamb. It is now up to you to keep your restoration.

A garden locked up, a place of secret delights in his mind. Wonderful, tantalizing things to discover. He was looking forward to the day when he could taste the fruit of her love. To tap into her passion and feel it pour over him. My, my! This gives us a hint to the next thing that causes a man to value a woman. Her mystery. Has anyone ever told you the end of a movie before you got to see and experience it for yourself? Kind of ruined it for you, didn't it? Well, when you give all that you have, including your body, too soon, it makes the love experience anticlimactic. It takes the fun out of it. It also decreases your value and his interest.

This same woman had brothers who asked her in Song of Songs if she was a door or a wall. If she was a door and had let other men enter her, they would enclose her in cedar, which was symbolic of putting her to death! But if she was a wall, keeping herself and not allowing any man into her, they would honor her with a tower of silver. You see the difference in value? One was worthy of discarding, the other was worthy of great reward in their eyes. She proudly proclaimed that she was a wall, her breasts were like towers because she could hold her head high with no shame. She brought contentment to her fiancé because she could be trusted.

Want to get a man? Allow him to see the Holy Spirit at work in your life. Attract him with godliness. Leave it to his own imagination to take him to places that you cannot. Want to keep a man? Keep the garden gate locked until he has committed in the sight of witnesses to tending all that the garden holds.

Intimate Choices

Do you not know that your bodies are members of Christ himself?
Shall I then take the members of Christ and unite them with a
prostitute? Never! Do you not know that he who unites himself with
a prostitute is one with her in body? For it is said, "The two will
become one flesh." But he who unites himself with the Lord is one
with him in spirit. Flee from sexual immorality. All other sins a
man commits are outside his body, but he who sins sexually sins
against his own body. Do you not know that your body is a
temple of the Holy Spirit, who is in you, whom you have
received from God? You are not your own; you were bought
at a price. Therefore honor God with your body.

1 CORINTHIANS 6:15-20

Some straight facts about your body. First, your body will never belong to just you. Right now it belongs to God. He paid for it. If you marry, your body will belong to your husband. When you've been left to look after something that belongs to someone else, it requires extra care. No one wants to present an article that has not been well kept back to its owner. Treat your body as if it is priceless—because it is. When visiting a museum, priceless articles are kept either under glass or heavily guarded. A sign usually warns, "Do Not Touch." The oils from the touch of observers would leave a residue on the painting or piece that would alter it and cause wear over time and decrease its value. In order to preserve the piece and ensure that its value appreciates, admirers must behold it from afar.

Second, you are bonded to whomever your body belongs to. It's called a soul tie. We are bonded to God through our union with Him through Christ Jesus. All that we are and all that we have belongs to Him. This is why, in His eyes, fornication is adultery. You are giving your body to someone who He has not chosen to love you in a committed marriage.

When you give your body to a man, you are now bound to him. If God is not the glue in the relationship, at some point in time the fragile bond you share in the flesh will break, leaving your spirit shattered. Because indulging in sexual intimacy is your choice, you do damage to yourself. After a soul tie is broken, you feel what is called in medical terms "phantom pain." This describes the sensation one feels after a person has had a member of their body severed or removed. This is what happens within the sexual union. Two become one in body and spirit. When one decides to leave, they are actually severing a portion of the other's spirit. The pain is excruciating and felt for endless teary nights.

If this is where you are right now, accept the reality of the pain and give it to God. Understand that weeping may endure for a night but joy comes in the morning. Hold out for healing, do not try to reattach yourself to this person in order to stop the ache. This will only bring greater pain later. There is no shortcut around the healing process. Walk with God, who is able to soothe and heal the frayed edges of your spirit and emotions. Keep pouring out your sorrow to Him until He's got it all. Keep your eye on the light at the end of the tunnel and take it one day at a time until you reach wholeness.

Third, you are not alone in the house called your body. The Holy Spirit resides there. He is involved in whatever you do with your body. Intimacy without consent is a violation. The Holy Spirit will never consent to sex outside of marriage. Keep this in mind and choose not to go against His wishes or grieve Him by dragging Him into something that is not pleasing to

Him. This is a touchy subject (pardon the pun), but we must be sober in the days to come as weariness threatens to set in and temptation increases. This is about self-preservation and joyful living. Have a made-up mind not to compromise yourself. It's never worth the price tag.

Remember that whomever you yield to, you become their slave. Yielding is an act of worship. For those not in a relationship at this present time, make up your mind not to be bonded to a man until he has made the commitment to be bonded to you in marriage. Until then walk like a well-kept woman who understands that her body belongs to a King and knows no one is deserving of her crown jewels until they've paid the price.

Real Talk About the "S" Word
(You got it, sex!)

1. God created it, Satan perverted it.

2. As noted relationship expert P. Bunny Wilson would say, "Sex is good when it is saved sex." That means God sits at the foot of your bed and applauds your union in the marriage bed, releasing you to be naked and unashamed in your celebration of love.

3. Sex before marriage negatively affects the trust factor after marriage. Self-control builds trust in one another's character.

4. Self-gratification will make it more difficult for your partner to please you. He will never be able to duplicate what you cause your body to grow used to.

5. Don't start anything that you shouldn't finish because you most likely will.

6. Oral sex, as the title suggests, is sex in case you were wondering. It is not an option for you as you wait.

7. Not only will you create a soul tie with anyone you have sex with, you will also create a physical dependency that might be stronger than your emotional pull to him. Therefore, you will keep returning to a man you don't even like because you are physically hooked. See the deception and cut the cord.

8. Intimacy without commitment is not a promise. It is a lie.

How to Handle Raging Hormones

*Offer your bodies as living sacrifices, holy and pleasing
to God—this is your spiritual act of worship.*

ROMANS 12:1

The answer is simple. Press into a deeper place of worship with the Lord. For everything in the natural, there is a spiritual parallel. God would not leave you lacking in anything. What is sex? What is worship? They are both the act of giving all that you are and all that you have to the one that you love. Worship is the act of forgetting about yourself and focusing completely on God, the first and most important object of affection. As you seek to please His heart in worship and praise, delighting yourself in Him, all you lack will be forgotten. True and satisfying worship is where you reach out for more of Him to fill the empty places inside yourself. Our longing for love, for fulfillment, for peace, for joy, for greater intimacy—these desires are satisfied the closer we draw to Him. In drawing closer, we learn more of Him. And truly to know Him is to love Him. But it goes even deeper than this.

In the King James Version of the Bible, when referring to a godly sexual union, it repeatedly says, "and he knew her," speaking of deep intimacy where two are naked and unashamed, hiding nothing, being completely vulnerable and transparent to one another. "Adam knew Eve and she conceived." When we "know" God, we make ourselves vulnerable and transparent before Him in praise and worship, pouring out all that is within us to Him. We conceive of the fruit of the Spirit and proclaim Christ and His characteristics to the world.

That's the spiritual side of it. The natural side of why I encourage you to worship when you wake up in the middle of the night and you feel as if your body is attending a party you didn't know you were invited to is because worship redirects your thoughts. The body must submit to the mind. We need to bring every imagination captive and submit our thoughts to the Lord. When we do this, He fills our minds with peace, fulfillment, and satisfaction. The flesh will then be quieted. Why? Because the glory of God will overshadow the demands of the flesh as we turn our thoughts heavenward toward the Lover of our souls and surrender all our desires to Him.

Therefore, in your singleness, give it all to God. There is a place you can go to worship where you find yourself spent, but satisfied. Completely overcome with the fullness of His Spirit in intimate communion. Reach higher, dig deeper, stay in His presence longer, and let Him cover and fill you with His love. Then rest in His arms and let your sleep be sweet.

Get Your Own Man

But since there is so much immorality, each man should have his own wife, and each woman her own husband.

1 CORINTHIANS 7:2

I am going to place a different emphasis on this scripture. Each woman should have *her own husband*, not anyone else's, *her own*. I am going to hit this quickly and move on. The big "A" word, *adultery*, is a big no, no, not ever! I am saddened to see this going on in churches across the land. Women coveting other women's husbands, praying for their demise. I'm sure you don't know anyone like this, but I am sad to say I do. I have one thing to say: "Stop it!" You are treading on dangerous ground and heading straight toward excruciating heartbreak and disgrace.

The excuses are countless for how many a good sister finds herself in this spot. First, your own vulnerability is at an all-time high. The devil has convinced you that due to the man shortage your husband is in prison or already married. It ain't necessarily so. Just because you haven't seen him doesn't mean that he doesn't exist. Next, some nice married man begins to give you the attention you've been longing for. He begins to share the problems he is having with his wife. He paints a terrible picture of his tortured, loveless existence with this woman. You think to yourself, *He's just not happy. He's merely existing in a marriage that has long been over.* Puh-leeze! This line has been used so much, it is not just tired, it is *exhausted*. For everyone

I've counseled, the line has been the same. Then the enemy comes whispering that this married man deserves better and *you* are that something better. You would know how to love him the way he needs to be loved...the rest is history. So here we go...

Tips on how to avoid falling into adultery:

1. Know your own vulnerability.

2. Walk in accountability with a trusted and godly friend who will speak the truth in love to you.

3. Do not entertain married men in close quarters or intimate settings.

4. Do not allow intimate conversations with married men.

5. If you cannot be friends with his wife, you cannot be friends with him. The two are one whether they like one another or not.

6. Do not entertain negative conversations about his wife. If he confesses problems to you, refer him to a godly brother. You will quickly see how interested he is in solving them.

7. Remember that when a man has an unfaithful spirit toward his wife, he will also be unfaithful to you. Even if you manage to capture him for a while you will always live with the torment of not being able to trust him completely.

8. You must agree with God that adultery is sin and highly offends the One who loves you most. It displays a lack of trust on your part for His ability to provide love and a companion for you.

9. Remain watchful over your own emotions and don't ignore the red flags that the Holy Spirit waves.

Want to be happy and stay happy?
Be patient and get your own husband.

Missionary Dating

Do not be yoked together with unbelievers. For what do
righteousness and wickedness have in common?
Or what fellowship can light have with darkness?

2 CORINTHIANS 6:14

*I*f you were dating someone and he didn't like your
mother, father, child (if you have one), or best friend who
had been with you through thick and thin...*a-a-a-and*
was not even interested in impressing them for your sake,
would you feel good about pursuing a relationship with this
man? Then how could you want to be in a committed relationship with a man who has no interest in God? What do you have
to share between you? If God is truly an integral part of your
life, this could definitely limit your conversation because you
would not have a lot in common. It would be like being a
tourist in France and not speaking French. You would not have
a very enjoyable vacation without the ability to communicate.
Conversation is key to intimacy. It is part of the experience of
"knowing" the fullness of a person. If your exchange is limited,
how close can you really get?

True joy is found in relationships that provoke you to higher
heights in Christ and deeper depths of personal growth. This
can only happen when both people are reading from the same
book. Otherwise you will have conflict, distraction, confusion,
and disappointment. It is like mixing linen and cotton together.
They pull against one another and ruin the shape of the outfit.

One has a looser weave. It doesn't have the same amount of strength to withstand wear.

I watched two strong healthy men the other day walking a very aged, bent-over woman across the street. These two men, who literally formed a yoke to support this dear lady, were reduced to walking at a snail's pace because of her weakened condition. That is the problem with being unequally yoked. The stronger has to suffer for the weaknesses of the other. The weak one is just...well, weak. He will not be pulled or stretched beyond what he is capable of doing with his own strength.

So you marry an unbeliever, thinking it will be fine. All of a sudden, now that you are married, you want to strengthen your relationship with God. He's not buying it. You want to go to church. He's not going for it. You want to tithe. He's definitely not going for that! You have children. They are confused. Why do they have to go to church if Daddy doesn't have to? Meanwhile, you hit every prayer chain you can to implore others to pray for your husband's salvation. You are married but your loneliness kills the joy of it all. It's happened too many times to count. At the end of the day, I have to ask you how deep is your love for Christ if intimacy with an unbeliever is not uncomfortable for you. You cannot serve two masters—you will love one and despise the other.

The Bible tells us that men and women ruin their lives with their foolish choices and then are angry with God. Joyless and frustrated, they wonder why God "allowed" this or that to happen. He allows you to exercise the free will He gave you, but He is hoping you love and trust Him enough to be obedient to His Word, to believe He knows what's best for you. Just as you can't bank on money that is not at hand, you cannot count on that man changing. Missionary dating is not the answer. You cannot save him. Wait on the Lord and (again I say) wait for the man He has chosen for you.

No Compromise

If you are completely sold out for Christ and able to stand firm in your convictions, you can be a mighty influence in an unsaved man's life. This only works, however, if you keep your standard of godliness intact. I personally have had several male friends in my life who were unsaved when we first met. I firmly believe that God allows people into our lives for a purpose, so I did not cancel them out, but neither did I embrace them. I continued walking toward the Lord, figuring they would either join me or grow weary of the journey. They hung around until they figured out that I was not going to compromise myself, and then they settled into being great big brothers and supportive friends. All of these men are now mightily saved and point to me as the catalyst for their conversion. This is your calling as a woman of God, to be a light to all who walk in darkness, including men.

I also have several friends who had unsaved men in their lives that they refused to compromise for. Their refusal to be less than what God had asked them to be catapulted their men into the arms of Jesus, so determined were they to win these ladies' affections. They agreed to being mentored by other godly brothers and grew in the Lord by leaps and bounds. They are now happily married. But again, the key here is *not* compromising your walk with the Lord!

Warning: If you know you cannot be strong, do not try this at home. Again I say: Wait on the Lord to send you a man after His own heart.

Women struggle with men because

they want men to be like them.

They are not.

The struggle would end if

we could learn to see our differences

as challenges to our own personalities.

Get on Board

Now I want you to realize that the head of every man is Christ,
and the head of the woman is man, and the head of Christ is God.

1 CORINTHIANS 11:3

For a man indeed ought not to cover his head, forasmuch as he is
the image and glory of God: but the woman is the glory of the man.

1 CORINTHIANS 11:7 KJV

One more reason to hold out for a man who is saved. If a man is to be the head over me, I definitely want him to be able to hear from God, don't you? You want a man who not only hears from God but also obeys Him. That will make your life a lot easier on all levels. If he hears and obeys God, then he will love you and lead you the way he should. You will have no problem submitting to him because you trust his judgment. Because you submit, he will love you more and do more things to please you. It is an endless circle of love when everyone is in the right place with God.

If you are presently experiencing problems with the other "S" word (that would be *submission*), you need to clear that up now before you get married. Understand there is nothing passive about submission. It is an active decision on your part to walk in cooperation with your partner, your boss, your father, your pastor, the person in line in front of you, the stop sign…we submit a hundred times a day without thinking about it and then get crazy when asked to submit to the one we supposedly love. Submission puts you in the position to be blessed, to get where you want to go in life, and avoid needless collisions. To submit to your husband is to submit to Christ. Do it in obedience to His Word, and He will bless you for it even when it is not noted by your partner.

Once submission is in place in a marriage, both people flourish in the relationship. The woman is happy and thriving, which makes her husband look good. She is his crowning glory, the evidence of his work well done. When the man looks good, then God looks good as the world looks on two people who are manifesting the glory of God through a beautiful partnership. As we consider submission in this light, it becomes a bigger issue than saying, "Yes, dear." It is about living your life to the glory of God.

A Woman of Value

A wife of noble character who can find? She is worth far more than rubies. Her husband has full confidence in her and lacks nothing of value. She brings him good, not harm, all the days of her life.

PROVERBS 31:10-12

Adam named his wife Eve, because she would become the mother of all the living.

GENESIS 3:20

Never underestimate the value of a woman. Never underestimate how much a man will appreciate you if you are on your mark. Funny, her looks are never mentioned in the dissertation on the Proverbs 31 woman, but her qualities are. She is called many things: noble, virtuous (which means excellent), valuable, a safe haven, an organizer, a homemaker, a hardworker, successful businesswoman, kind, gracious, giving, nurturing, inspiring, on and on. And after praising all of her virtues, her husband blesses her. Her children bless her. There is no doubt who the wheel in the middle of the wheel is at their house. She was not superwoman, but she was prized in the eyes of her family.

In spite of Eve's drastic mistake of serving the wrong fruit for dinner, and despite what it cost her and Adam, he still saw her potential and chose to bless her and give her a name of honor: "mother of all living things" or "life-giver." The memory of better days before the Fall had already cemented her image in his mind and caused him to love her no matter how she had trespassed. She had brought new life to his world when she entered it. That image could never be challenged no matter how many difficult times they would go through. She was his light and his glory. She truly was God's gift to this man.

What do you want the man in your life to call you? Work toward becoming that woman in preparation for the one who God brings. Cultivate your gifts as a woman from the inside out. Grow in wisdom and grace. The Proverbs 31 woman did not become an amazing woman overnight. She dealt with each season of her life by applying herself fully to it and understanding her purpose in the moment in which she lived. She used each season to her benefit to become a woman that her family would bless. As a single woman, you have the awesome opportunity to do the same.

Now should not be a sad or idle time. It should be a time of great investment in your future. Use it wisely, redeem the time joyfully, sow practical and spiritual seeds in your garden, and expect a rich harvest. You too will rise up one day and be called blessed by the man you love if you prepare yourself now.

Just Passin' Through

No longer will they call you Deserted, or name your land Desolate. But you will be called Hephzibah, and your land Beulah; for the LORD will take delight in you, and your land will be married.

ISAIAH 62:4

So you've wandered through the Desert of Singleness, stumbled up the Mountains of Loneliness, and back down to the Valley of Despair, meandered past Brooks of Hope run dry, and grown weary from the journey. How does one find her way to a place called Happy? By looking up, not forward. The future is not yours to see until the Lord chooses to reveal it. Therefore, keep your eye on the One who knows all things. The One who has covered you with His own banner of love and delight.

You are no less lovable just because you are not married. Kill that lie. You are not deserted. You are surrounded by the Most High. Your status does not make you who you are, only what you are called by God. He separates your name from the place where you live. You are a spirit who has a soul that lives in a body. Your spirit is merely passing through the land. The body will pass away and so will marriage when we stand before Him in heaven. How can we spend an entire lifetime obsessing over something so temporary?

You are the delight of the Lord. The more you tap into feeling that delight, the more delightful you will feel. His presence and love will become real to you and fill you to the point, where

I dare say, you will become rather ambivalent on the topic of marriage. *"Do I want to or not?"* you will ask yourself. *"I'm not really sure."* You will have to give pause for the thought, because once you discover what peace and joy really feels like, you hesitate to introduce anything into your life that might have the slightest potential to spoil it. I'm a witness that you can actually swing to the other extreme.

I have had people tell me they think I'm just a little *too* happy being single for my own good! However, I feel that this is exactly where God wants us to be. Reveling in the fact we are His beloved. We are His betrothed. Delight in His occupation of our land. We belong to someone from the inside out. Our natural status on the earth has nothing to do with who we are! You better get a clue on how desirable you are and walk in that thing, girl! It's time to get real, get free, and get happy! So slay the idol of marriage. Get over it. Then, when the right man comes along, you can really get into it because you will see exactly where you are going and be able to find your way there safely and joyfully.

The Perfect Scenario

Jesus is the Lover of your Soul,

loving you from the inside out.

The man in your life is

His glorious finishing touch...

Some Final Thoughts
on Happiness...

But godliness with contentment is great gain.
1 TIMOTHY 6:6

15 Secrets to Experiencing True Happiness...Better Known as Joy

1. Happiness is external, joy is internal and comes directly from God.

   Do not grieve, for the joy of the LORD is your strength. (Nehemiah 8:10)

2. The word of God fills our heart with joy. Following His word cleanses us from guilt and shame. His clear direction leads us to the path of joyful living.

   The precepts of the LORD are right, giving joy to the heart. The commands of the LORD are radiant, giving light to the eyes. (Psalm 19:8)

3. The Holy Spirit surrounds us and keeps us centered in kingdom living—pleasure and joy. Because we are in right relationship with God, we have peace which is always accompanied by joy.

   For the kingdom of God is not a matter of eating and drinking, but of righteousness, peace and joy in the Holy Spirit... (Romans 14:17)

4. Trusting in the Lord increases our joy because we are at peace with God and His intentions toward us. The Holy Spirit continually encourages us as we wait for all that God has in store for us.

May the God of hope fill you with all joy and peace as you trust in him, so that you may overflow with hope by the power of the Holy Spirit. (Romans 15:13)

5. Joy comes from feeling you've accomplished something at the end of the day. From reaping your harvest. Seeing the seeds of hard work and labors of love bearing fruit.

   For the Lord your God will bless you in all your harvest and in all the work of your hands, and your joy will be complete. (Deuteronomy 16:15)

6. Joy comes from knowing that your loving obedience brings pleasure to God and intimacy with Jesus. When He draws close, He fills us with His joy.

   As the Father has loved me, so have I loved you. Now remain in my love. If you obey my commands, you will remain in my love, just as I have obeyed my Father's commands and remain in his love. I have told you this so that my joy may be in you and that your joy may be complete. (John 15:9-11)

7. Joy comes from answered prayer. The secret to answered prayer? Praying in the will of the Father. The secret to praying in the will of the Father? Tapping into His heart, mind, and will through sweet and intimate communion.

   Until now you have not asked for anything in my name. Ask and you will receive, and your joy will be complete. (John 16:24)

8. Joy comes from fellowship with other believers who have the same witness as yourself about Jesus.

   We proclaim to you what we have seen and heard, so that you also may have fellowship with us. And our fellowship is with the Father and with his Son, Jesus Christ. We write this to make our joy complete. (1 John 1:3-4)

9. In the midst of God's awesome presence there is joy. Everything else is diminished in light of all that He is—trouble, lack, life and its pressures—all seem strangely inconsequential.

Splendor and majesty are before him; strength and joy in his dwelling place. (1 Chronicles 16:27)

10. When we see God as He is, we will discover the true source of pleasure—Jesus. When we see Him, our joy will be complete.

You have made known to me the path of life; you will fill me with joy in your presence, with eternal pleasures at your right hand. (Psalm 16:11)

11. In this world, we will have sorrow and tribulation, but these are the prerequisites to recognizing and experiencing true joy. No pain, no gain.

Those who sow in tears will reap with songs of joy. (Psalm 126:5)

12. God collects all of our tears and pours them out to make streams in the desert of our hearts. As we lift our voices in worship to Him, the path to joy becomes clearer.

The LORD will surely comfort Zion and will look with compassion on all her ruins; he will make her deserts like Eden, her wastelands like the garden of the LORD. Joy and gladness will be found in her, thanksgiving and the sound of singing. (Isaiah 51:3)

13. Not feeling joyful right now? This too shall pass. As you wait on Him through your season of weeping, His promise to you is sure and you can expect Him to do as He has said.

He will yet fill your mouth with laughter and your lips with shouts of joy. (Job 8:21)

14. Peace is the precursor to joy. It is the place of release to celebrate that all in your world is settled. Don't give your heart permission to be anxious. The end—by God. Therefore get happy, God's got it!

Peace I leave with you, my peace I give unto you: not as the world giveth, give I unto you. Let not your heart be troubled... (John 14:27 KJV)

15. The ultimate joy is in knowing that you are beloved and be-
    trothed. It is simply a matter of time for the manifestation.
    God's love for you is unending. It cannot be interrupted. It
    cannot be stolen. He will always be faithful, even when you
    are faithless. He longs to fill your every desire and make you
    wholly complete in Him. Begin to thank God ahead of time,
    praise ushers in the blessing of joy.

> *There will be heard once more the sounds of joy and glad-
> ness, the voices of bride and bridegroom, and the voices of
> those who bring thank-offerings to the house of the LORD,
> saying, "Give thanks to the LORD Almighty, for the LORD is
> good; his love endures for ever."* (Jeremiah 33:10–11)

Have you noticed in all of these meditations that a man was
never the source of joy? It's not about you, it's not about them,
it's all about Him. Your fiancé, Jesus. Preparing for a wedding
day on high! As you wait in joyous expectation on Him delivering all that He has promised, through the partnering of His
Word and your faithful obedience, joy will come and attract all
that you desire without all of the wearisome labor. God will
wipe away your tears and fill your mouth with laughter, laughter that will be contagious. Then your joy will be complete,
'cause you'll be downright happy from the inside out. This
thing called joy can become a habit if you are consistent in your
walk as a single person. Soon others will notice the change in
you and they won't be able to resist asking, "Girl, you sure are
looking sassy and satisfied these days... Aren't you still single?
How did you get so happy?" And you, in turn, will flash your
most brilliant smile and say, "Ooo, I'm so glad you asked me
that, have I got news for you!"

Aaahh joy...

> *the world can't give it and*

> *the world can't take it away.*

Other Books by
Michelle McKinney Hammond

To correspond with Michelle McKinney Hammond,
you may write to her:
c/o Heartwing Ministries
P.O. Box 11052
Chicago, IL 60611
E-mail her at **heartwingmin@yahoo.com**
Or log on to her website at:
www.mckinneyhammond.com or **www.heartwing.org**

For information on booking her for a
speaking engagement:
Contact **Speak Up Speaker Services at**
1-800-870-7719